UNDER GEMINI
A PROSE MEMOIR
AND
SELECTED POETRY

D0555169

9.95

Miklós Radnóti
UNDER GEMINI
A PROSE MEMOIR
AND
SELECTED POETRY

TRANSLATED BY

Kenneth and Zita McRobbie

AND

Jascha Kessler

INTRODUCTION BY

Marianna D. Birnbaum

OHIO UNIVERSITY PRESS
ATHENS, OHIO

All rights reserved
Published in Hungary by Corvina Kiadó, Budapest
and by Ohio University Press, Athens, Ohio

Cover design by Ferenc Barabás
Illustrations by Sándor RácMolnár

Introduction and English translation
© 1985 by Marianna D. Birnbaum, Kenneth and Zita McRobbie,
and Jascha Kessler
© Fanni Radnóti, 1985
Printed in Hungary, 1985
Kner Printing House, Gyomaendrőd

Library of Congress Cataloging in Publication Data

Radnóti, Miklós, 1909–1944.
Under Gemini.

I. McRobbie, Kenneth. II. Kessler, Jascha
Frederick, 1929–   .   III. Title.
PH3321. R27A26 1985   894'.51113   83–23751
ISBN 0–8214–0763–5
ISBN 0–8214–0764–3 (pbk.)

For distribution in all English-speaking countries

CONTENTS

5

INTRODUCTION

MIKLÓS RADNÓTI

1909–1944

On June 23, 1946 a mass grave was reopened at Abda, a small village in Western Hungary. The event was not unique at this stage of Hungarian history. Hardly a day went by that the authorities of one region or another would not receive word that local people had come upon corpses or hastily covered graves in the fields. According to the findings of the preliminary investigations, approximately six hundred feet away from the Rába, a small river running through the area, inmates of a forced labor camp had been executed. The ensuing exhumation proved to be a rather difficult job: the corpses were partially decomposed and the coroners had to identify the dead and the time and cause of death on the basis of shreds of clothing and disintegrated scraps of paper. The coroner's report on corpse number 12 read:

A visiting card with the name Dr. Miklós Radnóti printed on it. An ID card stating the mother's name as Ilona Gross. Father's name illegible. Born in Budapest, May 5, 1909. Cause of death: shot in the head. In the back pocket of the trousers a small notebook was found soaked in the juices of the body and blackened by wet earth. This was cleaned and dried in the sun.

On the first page of the notebook there was a short text in Hungarian, Serbian, German, French and English. The latter reads "... contains the poems of the Hungarian poet Miklós Radnóti... to Mr. Gyula Ortutay. Budapest University lecturer ... Thank you in advance." It is followed by his last poems with a final entry dated October 31, 1944:

I dropped alongside him, his body rolling over,
already tightening, a cord about to snap.

Shot in the neck. You'll be finished off like this—
I muttered to myself—so just lie still.
Patience flowers into death now.
Der springt noch auf, spoken over me.
Mud and blood drying on my ear.

The death described was not yet his own, it was the last moment of Miklós Lorsi, a fellow inmate, a formerly celebrated violinist, to which the tragic simile, comparing the dying body to a taut string, alludes. The poem marks the last station on the poet's long march that started with his induction into the forced labor camp and ended in the mass grave at Abda.

It is one of four short pieces, each charting his last steps toward death and, at the same time, signaling his successive withdrawal from "participation" in life. They are generally referred to as *Razglednicas*, picture postcards in Serbo-Croatian, and indeed they provide a terrifyingly precise "pictorial" description of the horrors the poet had experienced in the last months of his life. Separate as they stand in their unique message, the *Razglednicas* are by no means unrelated to the rest of Radnóti's poetry. They have a particularly close emotive and textual contact with his longer poems (such as *Forced March* and *A Letter for the Spouse*) written during the same period, and together they render a final panorama of Radnóti's surroundings, depicting the devastation man and nature suffer in a ravaging war. The first one opens with the sounds of destruction and continues in an apocalyptic scene:

Thick, ferocious roar of cannon rolling up from Bulgaria,
slamming into the ridge, hesitating, then falling;
man, beast, cart and thought all jammed,
the road shies whining away, the maned sky gallops off.
Amid this roiling confusion you are fixed in me,
shining in my deepest consciousness, forever still
and mute as the angel admiring the destruction,
or the beetle lodging itself in the rotting tree.

The tools of death, and men and beasts to be killed, are equally active in the first part of the poem. The road rears up like a terrified horse and the metonymy is further developed as the sky's foaming clouds are made into its ruffled mane. The furious, uncontrolled elements of reality related in the first four lines are contrasted to the image of the poet's wife, cast on the "inner landscape" of his mind. But as opposed to a "real" picture of his beloved, his wife's image turns into that of an angel, remote as a statue, even her glow forever unattainable, something that belongs to a world that no longer exists, ethereal, alien, and enigmatic, a figure on the wall of a cathedral. The concluding simile, while returning to the pedestrian world of the beginning, evokes eternity, as do fossilized insects in amber. The poem forms two separate, four-line entities, a formal reflection of the separateness of the outside world from the inner world of the poet.

The same structure is discernible in the second *Razglednica*.

From here it's nine kilometers
to where stacks and houses are burning
and dumb, terrified peasants roost
puffing their pipes at the edge of the meadows.
Here the little shepherdess steps
on the pond, ruffling its surface,
and the curly flock leans over
the water's edge drinking cloud.

Starting with another precise, non-poetic statement about distance, the poem unfolds into two different landscapes. In the first, simple people, the victims of history, are depicted. Hopelessly and helplessly they watch the destruction of their land. They draw on their pipes, the peasants' mute, defenseless reply to centuries of exploitation. They wait and hope to survive it all. The counterpart to this image of sad impotence is an equally terrifying tableau of the "idyll of ignorance." The charming shepherdess of a Boucher or a Fragonard is one of the most horrifying images in Radnóti. She symbolizes man's unawareness of his fate; she is anything but a figure in an idyll. Her tender movement, the quiet rippling of the water, is a deliberate and bitter contrast to truth. Her fate too is sealed; but she knows no more about it than do the sheep drinking beside her. The two "picture postcards" present a frozen moment in time. There is no change taking place, the guns and the fire do not come closer, the peasants do not move, no storm blows over the peaceful pastoral scene at the lake. The poet is not in either of the pictures; he watches from aside, knowing that the water's mirror will break, and all will fall apart.

The third poem is a four-liner, composed in iambic pentameter, which would not render it in English. The translation offers a mixture of metrical feet instead:

> Bloody spittle froths from the muzzles of oxen,
> people piss blood,
> the company's stuck in foul, rank clots.
> Hideous death blowing overhead.

Although the poet is present, he is not singled out in the crowd. Men and objects no longer differ in this horrible landscape: the anthropomorphization of things and the reification of people is completed. Men and oxen bleed alike; the earth and the company exude the same stench of destruction. Four heavy lines render four stills: different aspects of the one large picture.

The fourth *Razglednica* contains far fewer poetic elements. It concentrates on the moment between life and death. There is no alliteration, and the single "poetic" sentence, "Patience flowers into death now" is but a terrible paraphrase of a Hungarian proverb: "Patience flowers into roses." There is a great deal of deliberate obscurity in the piece. Events and dialogue can be viewed as interchanging in the manner of a classical ballad. Yet, a close reading of the text reveals an inner monologue instead. In the first two lines the immediate past is described, "I dropped alongside him." The speaker is placed prostrate on the ground next to a dying victim. The presence therefore carries the memories of the previous seconds and forecasts a shared, terrible future. The next sentence is formulated in this limbo: the poet registers the cause of death of the other and predicts his own. The moment of "patience" (a horrid euphemism for death-fear) is not broken but extended even further by the German phrase coming from the "outside," "*Der springt noch auf,*" one of the executioners shouts. The shot to stop and silence him forever does not ring out: the last moment of life is eternally long. It reaches beyond the poem. The jerking motions of the other's death-struggle are only opposed by the finality of the statement in first person: "... Mud and blood drying on my ear."

Radnóti died at the age of thirty-five. In 1959, commemorating his fiftieth birthday, one of his closest friends said that "with his last words—meaning the German quotation—the poet acquitted his nation of the opprobrium of his murder." It is true that Radnóti, while martyred for his Jewish origins, wanted nothing more than to be a Hungarian poet who speaks for his country and who represents the best humanist traditions of his nation in a world that had turned savage and insane.

This volume will acquaint the English-speaking reader with a representative sampling of Radnóti's poetry, and with his only long prose piece, *Under Gemini*. The latter is a subjective experience of space and time, a collection of memories in which outer chronology is substituted and/or amended by an inner one. Real time is thus not destroyed but subordinated and augmented by subjective ordering, which also permits Radnóti to use events as real or as metaphoric. This allows him to establish an arbitrary scale of importance for his information, and create a personal model of reality. "Narrated time" is projected back to the past, to his earliest memories, and it assumes a temporary *presence* as the "time of narration" and, simultaneously, it is cast ahead in the future. Radnóti also takes advantage of the possibility of conceiving of truth and time as conditional entities which can be turned about, and especially "replayed," achieving a synthesis between actual and conditional behavior. He employs the same method in *À la Recherche*... whose title clearly connects the device with Proust, its foremost master. Indebtedness to Proust is also manifest in the subject, since the memoir's topic is the remembering of things past. The act of remembering is triggered by, or will trigger idiosyncratic, recurring stimuli, as it appears when Radnóti thinks of Ági, his kid sister:

"When she comes to mind I hear the cadence of a sentence, an excited little girl's voice uttering the sentence, and that's what sets me off. When I hear that voice, it is always evening and the lamp is lit. When I hear the voice, father is sitting at the table, shirt shining whitely beneath his unbuttoned, faded military tunic. The cadence of the sentence haunts me as I strive to make out the words. I bow my head and listen."

Radnóti's immediate family appears in *Under Gemini* in a peculiar order and, what is remarkable, the most developed portrait is the stepmother's. She is the only one whose role radically changes in the course of the memories, and Radnóti succeeds admirably in following this transformation. By the time the reader truly gets to know her, their deep attachment to one another is based on a new relationship, which still incorporates the old. The stepmother's face radiates warmth, lively intelligence, and also femininity. She is the most significant woman in the child's life. In his adult years, her role is taken over by Fanni, Radnóti's only real love.

His deep concern for the world notwithstanding, Radnóti was primarily the poet of the individual, and his private experiences make up a large part of his poetry. In 1935 he married Fanni, to whom some of the most beautiful love poems of modern Hungarian literature are addressed. Their text is interlaced with ingenious metaphors whose most generous source is nature. Nature's images are simultaneously the medium in which Radnóti's social and moral messages are delivered. This, although less obvious in his prose, is clearly discernible in his lyrical memoirs.

Under Gemini is a search for a better understanding of oneself through the prism of memories. Clarifying the issues of childhood, identifying and sorting out the real and the imaginary sufferings, liberate the poet in order to face the present, whose imminent problems loom large over the memories of the past. Freedoms, artistic and real, are important categories in the story, discussed by the poet and his French friend Jean Citadin.

"Childhood is a big thing"—say the characters, not only the two friends, but also strangers around them. It is never remembered, however, as a whole, but selectively, *pars pro toto,* by its taste, touch, or smell. So are the people populating the past: the uncle smells of wine, his wife of the kitchen, and the poet's stepmother of fresh soap. And, in turn, a sudden aromatic or tactile experience can evoke their entire being and the events connected with them.

It is not the epic quality that dominates *Under Gemini*. The impressionistic patches appear arbitrarily linked together into a collage which, nonetheless, allows for the discrete reading of each segment because it forms an individual unit with its own aura of influence. A case in point is the poet's discussion about art and aesthetics. The conversation starts about Cocteau, and Jean criticizes him for his "magician's tricks." The subject then broadens to "permissible" artistic devices, truth versus artistic truth, form, and the art of translation. Just as real conversations move on, so does this turn from the general principles to the immediate problems with which the participants deal. Radnóti brings up his own translation, Tibullus's *Detestatio belli,* on which he was then working. The conversation could stand on its own. Yet the choice of discussing Tibullus in 1939 reveals an inner pattern of memories which connect events beyond the recollections of childhood, emerging as the problem of war and violence, politics, and the pedestrian manifestation of the history of destruction. While past and present alternate in the volume, politics always intrude and prove to be as powerful as the most intimate personal causalities in their lives.

It is, however, important to keep in mind that, despite his tragic fate, Radnóti was not an entirely pessimistic poet. There are scores of playful, happy pieces in his œuvre, and many of them were written in Paris or reflect the carefree mood of his trips abroad. Although not included in this selection, Radnóti first appeared with avant-garde poems, and his literary influences were primarily the avant-garde poets of France. The heavy cadence known from his later, classical period does not reveal the light-hearted, modernist images present in some of his early verse. His stylistic road—leading in the opposite direction to what is usually the case—is another proof that Radnóti's language did not conform to any literary fashion, but rather to the grave times in which he wrote. Yet, some of his unexpected metaphors, bold similes and disjointed images allude to his avant-garde beginnings.

Radnóti's childhood, his questions about freedom and the

meaning of his life reappear in the *Fourth Eclogue*, in which
Jean Citadin's parallel becomes the inner "voice":

POET
If only you'd asked me as a fetus...
I knew, O I knew!
Shouting, It's barbarous! Don't want life!
Pounded dim in the dark, and slashed by light!
And I've made it. Head's been hard a long time.
All that bawling merely exercised my lungs.

VOICE
And red waves
of measles and scarlatina tossed you ashore.
The lake once tried to gulp you—and coughed you up.
Why do you suppose time has taken you in its arms
                                                    after all?
and heart, liver, winged lungs,
that slimy, mysterious machinery
goes right on working...

Among the poems, his *À la Recherche...* is a collective fare-
well to dead friends and to a human existence passed. In turn,
his eight eclogues are his literary and private testament for
posterity. In them he described and responded to the devastat-
ing events of his time and, although rarely, expressed his hope
in a better future to come after his murder. Considering the
information couched in these poems, it is highly interesting
that Radnóti chose such an unexpected vehicle, and that this
bucolic genre became the carrier of his unhappy message.

The eclogue, a conventional, usually pastoral poem, is
generally structured in the form of a dialogue. The term was
first applied to Virgil's bucolic poems, and the technique was
later used by such poets of the Renaissance as Dante, Petrarch,
and Boccaccio. By the eighteenth century its themes broad-
ened, and town life, politics, war became fashionable eclogue
topics. Nonetheless, it has remained primarily a "choice
poem," in which shepherds are introduced conversing in an
idyllic atmosphere.

There is a deep affinity between Virgil and Radnóti regarding the purpose in writing their eclogues. As the modern interpreters of Virgil claim, "at the time of an inhuman world of brute force, Virgil built up his own Arcadia, in order to escape into it..."

In 1938, a short-lived periodical, the *Argonauts,* appeared. It folded after three issues, but in each of them Radnóti had either a poem or a translation published. One of the latter was the *Ninth Eclogue* of Virgil. As is known, the *Ninth Eclogue* was composed during the Civil War and Virgil's fear of the future and feelings of defenselessness are clearly felt in it. Radnóti's eclogues are a series of "destroyed idylls." Yet, for him *to live* was identical with *to create,* and as long as there was the remotest chance to write, that, and *only* that, was the obligation of the poet. Each eclogue contains a statement about this commitment. In the *First Eclogue* the poet confesses:

I write anyhow, living at the heart of this insanity
like that oak tree: it knows it'll be cut down, and though
that cross blazed on its trunk bleaches and says the ax
clears this ground tomorrow, it puts new leaves out just
the same...

The same "compulsion" is reaffirmed in the *Second Eclogue.* When asked by the Pilot whether he had written anything since the day before, the poet answers:

I have. Something else I can do? The cat
miaows, the dog howls, and the little fish
lovingly lays its eggs. I set it all down on paper...

I write. Something else I can do? And how dangerous
a poem is, if you but knew, even one whimsical, delicate
line,
because it also takes guts, you know: poet writing, cat
miaowing, dog howling, and the little fish—etcetera...

In the *Third Eclogue,* written a couple of months later, the poet poses the question whether it is at all permissible to write about anything other than the tragic events engulfing the world. Is it not immoral to write about love?

15

Country Muse, help me! The poets of this age are dying
away...
the skies drop on us, no mound is raised above our ashes,
nor are they by noble, lovely Grecian urns sustained.
Yet if a poem or two of ours remains... may I write of
love still?
Her body radiates toward me—O Country Muse, won't
you help?

The traditional dialogue disappears in the *Third Eclogue:* the Muse does not respond. She returns in the *Fourth,* where the conversation takes place between the Poet and the Voice, namely, his own conscience. Written on March 15, 1943, it marks yet another anniversary of 1848 and carries a plea for freedom. "...Help me, freedom, to find my home at last!" Aware of his forthcoming death, Radnóti repeats his avowal:

I'll be free, the earth shall let me go,
the broken world above the ground burns
smoldering. The slates are smashed.
Heavywinged imagination, you're soar:

His plight gains cosmic dimensions from the image created by the inner voice's answer:

Though all things here be broken, may your fury
rise, and write on the heavens in smoke.

Yet there is a point when pain seems to be too intolerable and too sharp to be put into words. The *Fifth Eclogue,* dedicated to the memory of György Bálint, a friend who had "disappeared" in the forced labor camp, remained, and was subtitled, a *Fragment.* The loss of the close friend and the premonition about his own fate halts his pen: the thoughts are too terrible for Radnóti to contemplate to their logical end.

Missing in action. A blow, this news.
And the heart within thuds, freezing.
A bad, tense pain lodges between these ribs;
it quivers; the words you spoke long ago

16

are fresh in memory; I feel your bodily presence
like the dead—
    Yet I can't write about you today!

The *Seventh Eclogue* belongs to the final period in Radnóti's
œuvre, depicting life without humanity, an "anatomy of
horror." It is a lyrical monologue, written in a pointedly un-
lyrical language: the surroundings determine the vocabulary.
Yet amidst filth, indignities and death-fear, the concept of
home still appears in a literary metaphor, "... a land in which
this elegiac measure is understood." The need to write, to
communicate his sufferings, remains alive:

> Missing punctuation, just groping line after line,
> I scrawl poems here in the dusk just as I live,
> bleary, inching over the sheet like a caterpillar;
> torch, book, everything confiscated by the Lager
> guard, fog falling on the barracks instead of mail.

The last *Eclogue*, the *Eighth*, is based on a syncretic view of
the biblical and the bucolic myths. Here the shepherd of the
First Eclogue becomes a real prophet, the furious one of
Elkosh. He is still connected with *writing*: another prophetic
activity. Nahum is remembered by the poet by what he has
written ("Your archaic anger I know: your writing still
exists"). In turn the prophet is familiar with the poet's work:

> ... Your last poems I know. Anger keeps you alive.
> The prophet and poet's wrath are twin: meat and drink
> to the people...

Thus in his last *Eclogue* Radnóti returns to the concept of
literary Romanticism, to the messianic role of the poet.
There is no poem which is undisputedly identified as the *Sixth
Eclogue*.

For Radnóti the concepts of living and writing became iden-
tical even before the *Eclogues*. Although his ars poetica can
only be culled from incidental phrases scattered in his poetry,
the poet's commitment to the surrounding world is an ever-
present feature in his work.

Radnóti knew that he would not return to see a free and democratic Hungary. He had been anticipating his death ever since the Nazi takeover of Germany in 1933. But even when facing his immediate end, the paramount, gnawing question on his mind was not how to save himself but how to assure that his poems in the small notebook would not perish with him.

His poems survived and the following generations have been reading them ever since. They know them by heart, they teach them in the high schools and universities of Hungary. Scholars have been analyzing his work and rediscovering each piece with each new reading. There is always a hitherto unnoticed fine metaphor, a particularly successful harmony between sound and meaning that may surface with another close reading of the text. Additional ties between his poetry and that of his contemporaries are discovered by scrutinizing his vocabulary and the micropoetic components of his language. Like all great poets he is as inexhaustible for the interested reader as he is for the scholar. He perished young, but he achieved what he had desired most—he became an inalienable part of Hungarian literature. And as the years pass, he is more and more recognized on a European scale as a significant poetic witness to our time, ranking with the late Paul Celan and the Nobel-laureate Nelly Sachs.

The excellent translations by Kenneth McRobbie and Jascha Kessler will further contribute to his triumph over his murderers.

Marianna D. Birnbaum

UNDER GEMINI

A DIARY ABOUT CHILDHOOD*

* *Ikrek hava. Napló a gyerekkorról* (Budapest, Magyar Helikon, 1973).
First published in 1940.

Often in my thoughts these days is my little sister Ági. I haven't seen her for years. It has been a long time since she went to stay in a small town at the foot of a great black mountain, and now she's living with her husband in the far-off capital of a strange country. We love each other very much, so we hardly ever write letters. This love is so strong, it needs no proof through letters; during a year I'll write once or twice, and she five or six times. But we often think about each other, are often aware of each other. We know each other so well, though we were together for only seven or eight years at the outset of our lives, she being eight and I twelve when we were parted. Such an exciting childhood it was; war went its way, and around us revolutions danced.

We were living beside a large barracks where the guard was continually being changed, where trumpet-calls continually resounded. And ever new calls were being sounded. We lived near the great palace on whose steps, at every hour of the day come rain or shine, people were cheering, idling around, waiting, bowing and scraping, or else authority was pronouncing judgement. We were hanging around in history, playing among thick-lettered news headlines on the square in front of the palace.

Ági is more than ever in my thoughts these days, and when she comes to mind I hear the cadence of a sentence, an excited little girl's voice uttering the sentence, and that's what sets me off. When I hear that voice it is always evening and the lamp is lit. When I hear her voice father is sitting at the table, shirt shining whitely beneath his unbuttoned faded military tunic.

The cadence of the sentence haunts me as I strive to make out the words. I bow my head and listen.

"And then they cut off his head and put it in a chest!" That's the sentence, and it's Ági speaking. She's lying with enthusiasm, brown eyes widening excitedly above the white serviette tied round her neck. She is sitting up the highest, raised on two cushions above her plate. We glance at each other.

"In short, they shot him dead and then actually cut off his head, did they?" father asks smiling after a moment's silence. "Yes," Ági insists, "with such a long curved knife!" She is sitting with arms outstretched, looking as if she would ascend from her cushions; the lie lifts her, she is almost flying, glowing; in one hand she grasps the spoon, in the other a big thick pencil. The spoon drips milk-rice.

"She's lying! She's lying again!" I burst out roughly, recovering from my astonishment. Ági's stories always filled me with wonder, wonder that often kept the fury repressed, but now it burst out. For here was the lie taking shape before my eyes, a growing giant; I was witnessing not only the exciting continuation of its development, but the reality of artistic creation; the experience we shared had now almost disappeared, and this was what provoked me. I felt there was no truth to any of it. Ági had made it up. Had made it all up, and it's not even afternoon yet, and this isn't dinner we're having but only lunch. The afternoon had shattered me, and precisely for that reason was already lurking in the depths of my consciousness. It was the past, or not even the past any more; it existed in dream timelessness deep down among other hidden memories, from where it will slowly surface, composed of tiny flashes, flavors, fragrances, movements, and also of sounds, it is reconstituted from the sounds, once and for all, truly and forever. Of course, I could not know this at the time, but all of a sudden I took Ági's exaggeration very much to heart.

After lunch father had a headache and went to lie down. I wanted to go up to the third floor to play with buttons, but mother put me in charge of Ági. "Go on off to the square." She shooed us out, and shut the door on us.

"Lali!" I shouted bitterly. Lali appeared above me, his close-cropped head shone white as he leaned expectantly over the balustrade. "I've got to go out now," I called up. Not waiting for his reply, I clattered furiously down the stairs, two at a time. The buttons rattled in my pocket. Holding fast to the banisters, Ági clambered down panting after me. In the gateway she took my hand, blinking up at me happily, knowing that I have to stay with her, have to hold her hand, and that we have to go out to the square. A little maliciously, triumphantly glad, she was making the most of the situation.

As we set out for the square I gave her a shove toward the edge of the sidewalk, then one from the sidewalk down into the road. Ági clambered back up, struggled hard, fought back, and after a few steps more was down in the road again beside the sidewalk. She treated it as a silly little tiresome game, but I was getting my revenge and by the time we reached the square I had already calmed down. "Now, since we're here, we might as well play something," I thought to myself, making the best of it. Ági played happily. We collected flat pebbles with which we spelled out letters on one of the benches. We caught insects. The square was empty. We made our way across to the palace nearby, and with a sharp stone drew scratches on the steps.

The after-lunchtime silence suddenly hardened, then came approaching rhythmical sounds. Armed soldiers appeared on the square, marching in step, a tired bearded soldier in their midst;* in dirty uniform without a belt, and unarmed, he was keeping in step hemmed in among them.

A cloud swam in front of the sun, and it turned even warmer. We got to our feet and watched them. Ági stood a little behind me and held onto me. People came hurrying in our direction from the streets giving onto the square; a crowd gathered, standing in front of us, standing all around us. We couldn't see a thing.

I stood there, sweating. Something horrible was happening, I felt it. Heat poured from the clothes of the people around us. I looked up; the sky was grey.

And then Ági lets go of me and begins to wriggle, worming her way between legs. I shout after her, but she vanishes. She'd been entrusted to me; now she'd disappeared. "Always hold her hand, you're bigger than she is. You're a boy, take care of your little sister," a warm familiar voice said inside me. Terrified, I rush headlong after her, stepping on somebody's

* Probably a deserter at the end of World War I.

23

foot; someone strikes me on the head; murmuring, they pull at me from behind. At last, exhausted, I get to stand behind Ági and grasp her elbow.

The soldiers form up in close order in a short line at the foot of the broad stairs, their backs all looking alike; now they press their rifles in against their shoulders. The soldier with the beard is standing a little further up, his eyes blindfolded with a wide black scarf. There's a shout, detonations, white smoke eddying up. The man with the blindfold is still standing; then he falls to one knee, slumps forward, rolls down two stairs and remains lying there. Again more shouting. A man in striped brown coat and black leather trousers blocks the way. Ági wants to see. She grabs at him, trying this way to push him to one side. "Off with you!" someone growls, and they begin pressing us back.

We find ourselves on the fringe of the crowd, dishevelled and sweating. Ági glances excitedly up at me.

I take hold of her wrist, and we trudge back toward the square. We sit down on a bench. "Probably he was a gypsy who made off with children," whispers Ági, the story already taking shape in her mind. I don't reply; the sun is shining once again. A small cabbage-butterfly alights on Ági's skirt; she catches it, wings sticking to her little sweaty fingers.

Later on it got really cloudy, and so we made our way home, subdued. I raced up to Lali's and we played with buttons till evening.

Now the afternoon whirrs across the evening dinner-table once more. There were a thousand soldiers, red uniformed, sounding their trumpets, on the stairway stood the child-stealing gypsy; blood gushed all the way down to the benches. The lamp was swinging.

"She's lying! She's lying again!" I shrieked, the scream rising shrilly this time.

"Be quiet! Eat up now, and let's have an end of it! Ági, you've been a little pig, the tablecloth!" mother snaps at her. Ági hunches her shoulders, spoons up the milk-rice rapidly, clambers down from her chair, and goes to sit in the corner. She is dressing her doll, but meanwhile her eyes flash angrily at me. Suddenly Ági looks at me again and begins to shout, her voice rising to a shriek: "You are the liar! Not I! Liar,

24

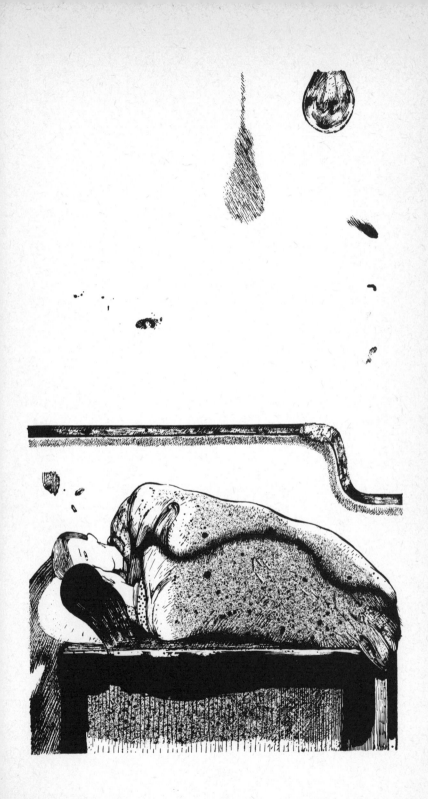

liar, liar!" Father winces. "If we don't have quiet here this instant!... If you dare answer her!"

I say my thanks for the dinner, and curl up in a corner of the sofa. For weeks I've been reading a book of war stories. The cover depicts seven soldiers standing around a wooden cross shrouded in snow, bareheaded, with snow on their shoulders. They are weeping; but the book has some cheerful stories too, and these are the ones I like, the others terrify me. Soldiers mistaking the full moon as it rises for an airship, and shooting at it—that's what one of the stories is about. And there's another tale of comic misunderstanding. A bear has stuck his head out from some bushes while he was licking honey; they take him for a fur-capped Cossack and surround the spot, and when they find out their mistake, collapse laughing on the grass. Meanwhile the bear ambles off. I'm poring over this account again, but somehow can't concentrate. I leaf nervously past the more gory ones; for a moment I think about my Petőfi*, but can't be bothered to get it. I just sit, and something is restless within me, some undefined anxiety.

By now the table is bare, from out in the kitchen there's the clattering of plates as mother washes up. This is the only sound, with father now and again turning a page of his paper, and Ági whimpering over her dolls. And I seem to hear the current running through the wire along the wall, seem to hear the light buzzing in its bulb. That's what I'm listening to.

Mother comes in from the kitchen, glances at father, takes off her apron, and begins arranging things for the evening. I have to help make up the bed. I fold up the lace coverlet smelling of dust, and together with mother distribute the cool bedding. The room's aspect changes. Ági is hanging around me, but doesn't look my way. She shows she's angry with me; she's waiting for us to make up. We get ready for bed without uttering a sound. No throwing our little pillows, no splashing about during the evening wash.

I am lying down in the dusk, one of the street lamps is shining in just a bit. I am playing with the fringe of the sofa, as I always do before falling asleep. It's because of the curtains

---

* Sándor Petőfi (1823–1849). Killed in battle. One of the greatest Hungarian poets, who adopted realistic themes and believed that freedom is the most important part of human happiness.

that I don't look in the direction of the windows. Not that I'm scared any more; but all the same, I don't look at them.

This is the hour when the street and the inner courtyard step with their sounds into our room. A streetcar turns by the distillery at the corner, ringing its bell, the door of the tavern opposite us opens, with strident sounds of singing and music; then with a sudden scream everything falls silent like when a needle slurs into the middle of a record while it's playing. Footsteps echo, a car squeals. In the courtyard there's clopping of slippers, jingling of keys, the gate opening, gate closing, people walking, walking on the staircase and in the passageway. The sounds rock me; now here and now there they pluck at me, lift me up, envelop me. I sleep, but only fitfully.

"Are you sleeping?" I hear Ági's voice now; right after it a warm breath touches me, and I feel a moistness behind my ear. Ági's kiss.

"Come and play!" she whispers, and I sit up. She is standing beside the sofa in her little blue chemise; in the dusk her head is disproportionately large. I cannot see her eyes, but I feel that she is smiling as she asks.

"What shall we play?" I lean toward her.

"Whatever you like," she breathes, anxious to oblige.

Most of the light falls in the middle of the room beside the table. We sit facing each other on the floor, and begin taking out the pebbles we had collected that afternoon. Ági lays down a line, I another, and I get out my carefully hoarded buttons as well.

"Let's make every fifth one a button," I whisper, and Ági makes little contented sounds.

"Four pebbles, one button," she counts them out happily, feeling honored that she may touch the buttons. The lines grow longer as we crawl along the floor. Behind Ági stands a chair with father's coat hanging over the back. She seats herself a little further off, knocks against the chair, and the chair tips over. As it falls the bed in the other room creaks in alarm, and the lamp comes on above it.

"It was he knocked it over!" Ági screams in fear, not looking but only pointing at me. We stand annihilated in the shaft of light, big white circles growing ever bigger revolve

27

before my eyes. Mother is also growing bigger, her black eyes pierce us. She looms in the doorway's lighted rectangle; in her heavy white nightdress she is like an angry statue.

"Off with you to the firewood box!" For a second, mother's glance rests on me. "As for you, go to bed; I don't want to hear another sound! We'll go into it all in the morning!" Ági doesn't budge, large pearls slowly forming in her eyes.

I tuck the quilt and the pillow under my arm and go out to the kitchen. This is the worst of the summertime punishments. To sleep on the big hard woodbox in the kitchen with its food smells, where the water tap gives frightening gurgles and there are cockroaches too. It happens only rarely, and in the mornings I always wake up inside on the sofa; when I've fallen asleep, mother or father carries me in. But it's frightening all the same.

I clamber up onto the box, wrap myself in the eiderdown quilt, and turn toward the wall. I reach out to touch a spot, fearfully, to see whether it will run away. More frightened than angry.

"Off to bed with you!" mother shouts from within.

"No!" Ági's protest chokes off into a cry. The door opens, and I roll over onto my back. Ági trots in through the half-opened doorway with bare feet, head held high, dragging her quilt and pillow along the floor behind her. Whimpering, she climbs up onto the box beside me; with tiny moans she crumples the pillow under her head, her little moist nose presses against my side. I can feel the warmth of her body.

Inside, they turn off the light.

"The rascals stick together." Half asleep, I can hear how touched the voice is.

"Yes, together." I seem to hear the low answer after a long pause, but perhaps I only dream it.

THURSDAY. Four days ago mother arrived from N., where she has been living for some fifteen years. Her arrival was unexpected, she had come into some money. I go to meet her at the railway station, and when I see her at the door of the carriage I tell myself that she is beautiful still. I haven't seen her for five years, and she hasn't aged a bit. "She must be forty-seven, forty-eight," flashes through my mind. We kiss.

Behind her a man gets off; he sets down mother's hand-luggage, clicks his heels, and kisses her hand.

"Here's my son." Mother holds me at arm's length, and smiles at the man through her tears.

"I can't believe it," her traveling companion says, raising his hat to me. I nod sullenly; I'm jealous, just like when I was a child.

"You know, you wouldn't believe what lies this man was telling me, all the way from N. to Pest," mother confides laughingly in the streetcar.

"You shouldn't talk to strangers," I say with mock severity. "But please, teacher"—with a tiny movement she drops a curtsy, tucking one leg behind the other, bending her knees—"don't be angry," and she looks askance. I laugh. We arrive at the other railway station, for mother is going on to her brother Eduárd's, at V. "I shall go down there this week," I shout after the train as it pulls out.

And now I am on my way to V., with two books and a note-pad in my briefcase, hat and raincoat. I'm traveling. It almost counts as a journey, I'm even taking along a notepad, a childish dream of journeying. I take out one of the books from my case, stow various things up on the baggage rack, and settle down by the window.

I have come this far through alarming newspaper headlines; today Europe's fate will be decided again; I live in a state of excitement and also solemnity, but I'm beginning to get used to it. And the miraculous is more and more part of my life's reality.

I open the volume of French poetry at random and begin to read.

Terre Terre Eaux Océans Ciel.
*J'ai de mal du pays.**

Here's Cendrars howling in the autumn of 1919, that wild European who once collected into a volume the magical songs and stories of Negro tribes.

* Earth Earth Waters Oceans Sky
Homesick am I.

29

Je voudrais être la cinquième roue du char
Orage
Midi à quatorze heures
*Rien et partout.**

My ears are ringing from it, but I can just catch the voice.
There's a jolt, and a voice roars out: Soroksár! as if howling
from out of the poem. It's all the same, I smile to myself, war
is on its way, just one day off?—two years? I want to be free!
It was after the war that the poet had traveled like this.
Is there really an "after the war"? He went on his travels with
all the eagerness of a soul once condemned for four whole
years to death, with joy, and with the nerve-wracking aware-
ness that the frontiers could close around him at any moment,
and he'd be a prisoner once again.

I turn a few pages of the book. Here's Larbaud:

Je chante l'Europe, ses chemins de fer et ses théâtres...

I sing Europe, its railways and its theaters...
the siting of its cities, while
I bring to birth a new world in my poems...

Beautiful, that "new world," I murmur, then begin to smile.
Such a long time since I translated this poem, and still don't
know who that Ilanero is! "I have vanquished you, only to be
your slave, O Ilanero!" Ilanero... beautiful name. "*C'est
l'exotisme.*" I play the pedant. Certainly, after the war—why
then? Not now too? "Europe is the unknown jungle, abode of
man-eaters, head-hunters, snakes whistling under the bushes";
how romantic the journey born of restlessness. Not London,
Paris, Berlin; it was Budapest, Belgrade, Kharkov, Bucharest
caught their interest. And what did they care about *couleur
locale*! It's not scenery they need but consciousness, the con-
sciousness of journeying, more precisely the consciousness of
being free. In foreign parts they worked just as if they were at

* I'd like to be the vehicle's fifth wheel
  Storm
  Noon at 2 p.m.
  Nothing and everywhere.

home among their books, and at home as if in the very depths of the densest jungle. I'm talking about the soul's reality—correction, *they* are talking about it —which is by now independent of all other realities. And was it a slip of the pen a moment ago? I could speak of myself too. Have twenty years passed since then? Since then, everything has continued unchanged. Or has it now begun anew? O happy ancestors, noble Jack London and inoffensive Pierre Loti, this journey, this craving for freedom is no mere adventure; no adventure, no hunger for knowledge, renewal, or escape—no, it is more: it is psychosis.

Walls are going up all around me, towns and countries disappear. The wall is rising, cutting me off from whole peoples. I'm a prisoner. And if sometimes someone cries out "Europe!" it's as if he were shouting "Africa!"

"How pathetic of me," I think listlessly. I shut the book. Really, all I'd like to find out is whether the last train for Nogent still leaves Paris from Bastille at one twenty in the morning.

"Ilanero," I repeat; and "Taksony!" someone calls out from down below.

"Taksony," I murmur too. I get down and stand in the flying dust in front of the station. There's a wait for the bus. "Does it run to Bugyi* on weekdays too?" I ask a young girl. "Yes, but it doesn't go often," she blushes through the dust. "Ilanero." I look at the girl again. "You have fair hair, you can't be Ilanero. Ilanero is dark. Raven-black hair."

Taksony, I am looking at the station, its seven letters, seven... Tass, Töhötöm, Huba, Kond and old Álmos, Előd, the foolhardy Ond.** If the old leaders press on forward the rest will follow after... I'm doing scansion; almost unconsciously; when the dactyls assemble.

Eduárd is a trifle disappointed when he meets me.

"So you have come down after all? Couldn't you find anything better to do?" It turns out later that his prediction had been wrong, that's why he's put out. "He won't be coming down to see you, not before next week," he'd assured

---

* Bugyi. A village in Pest County. Its name means a girl's panties.
** The names of the seven leaders of the seven tribes of the Magyars at the time of the migrations.

31

mother. "Poets and their promises... he never so much as writes you a letter."

On the veranda, we shake hands.

"Ilka," he calls out in the direction of the kitchen garden, "your son's come down!" Mother hastens out in a red apron, her face tanned, guffawing behind her capers Kormos the sheepdog, he's the first to reach me; paws up against my chest he licks my face, mother can hardly get near me because of him.

"The welcome they give you! One would think you loved them." Eduárd blinks from an armchair.

"He does love us." Mother throws her arms around me. "We all love each other, Eddie."

"That's as it should be," Eduárd smiles archly, as he always does when he has succeeded in getting someone worked up. *Memory of Childhood*, a short poem from my latest book, is about him:

That here they might offer, never expect they would.
"Ask for yourself, the kitchen's to the right,"
a relative gives me heart, good old Eduárd.
And I ask, I wheedle, then holding a wheel-
shaped slice of bread dipped in dripping-fat
I walk around, and my swallowing aloud
*makes the hearts of the kitchen-girls grow soft.**

"You know, everyone will think that it's just for the sake of the rhyme that the name's brought in here like this," Fanni** said concernedly when I showed her the poem one evening. "But why? It really is his name," I smiled; "still, let's add something... now, wait a bit":

---

* Hogy kínáljanak itt, azt sose várd,
jobbra a konyha, kérj magadnak, –
bíztat rokonom, a jó Eduárd.
S én kérek, újra kérek s nagy kerek,
zsírba mártogatott kenyerekkel
settengek, és a konyha-némberek
szívét lágyítva hangosan nyelek.
** Fanni Gyarmati, whom Radnóti married in 1935.

Not Eddie,
Not Eddie,
Eduárd!
Who, in
Youth,
in Ameri-
*ca lived hard.**

"Oh," she laughed, "don't add a thing, I'd much rather believe it, and others will believe it too."

And indeed, out of the whole family it's only mother who calls uncle Eduárd Eddie. Ever since he came back home he has signed himself Eduárd, and everyone addresses him this way and loves him this way.

We sit facing each other on the veranda; our two wine-glasses are down beside our armchairs, and between us stands a bottle of light dry wine. We keep it there on the freshly sprinkled bricks because it stays cooler that way, and because Eduárd likes to put his feet up on the table, the garden table which is slightly lame and can easily tip over.

"And so let's talk a little about literature, too, family matters are a bore." Eduárd strokes his short beard. "How true are the rhymes cutting, young fellow? Are they cutting true now? Really cutting?"

"Cutting true, of course!" I murmur docilely, continuing to scratch Kormos's head.

"You'll end up full of fleas from that hound, for your information!" he says jealously. As if he understood what was behind the sentence, the dog gets to his feet sluggishly, goes across to Eduárd, and leans his head upon his knees. The two of them blink at me. Mother takes up position between us, watching us closely, ready momentarily to jump in to play the peacemaker.

"Don't be always teasing him; he's not just a poet, you

* Nem Ede,
  Nem Ede,
  Eduárd!
  Fiatal
  Korában
  Ameri-
  kában járt.

33

know. He's a teacher too! At least you'll grant that this is a profession, won't you? And it's not his fault, poor boy, that he hasn't got a proper job!"

"How many years has he been without one? Time enough to become a master cabinetmaker! Now, in the Yu-Es-Eh,* by now he'd... But I'm always squabbling with you, aren't I?" he laughs at me suddenly with sparkling, kind eyes.

"Do you remember," mother asks in the garden, "how you didn't like spinach? You hated it! Then from one day to the next you began to eat it, without having to be lectured or argued into it anymore! There it was! But once after lunch we noticed how fat your face was, all puffed out. You had stowed away the spinach in both cheeks, holding it in all through lunch. How you could chew on anything else is a mystery to this day. We laughed, your poor father and I! For a while after that, you used to have to stand in front of us and open your mouth, while we were bursting as we looked inside."

"I don't remember," I smile, "but what's this?"

Infernal clashing sounded from the house.

"That's the gong!" Mother bows ceremoniously, "Eddie's new toy, announcing lunch."

In a boy scout shirt and an enormous fraying brimmed straw hat, Eduárd stands on the stairs leading up to the veranda, whacking a sheet-iron lid with a wooden spoon. His short prickly fringe of beard glistening merrily.

"The soup awaits within," says he, bowing toward us.

He's always up to something. Now, however, only the sort of things which don't cost anything. It's twenty years since he returned from America and bought this small property, at quite a price, they say. The house was designed by Lechner**; Eduárd took a liking to it and bought it. Besides, it happens to suit him ideally. The overgrown garden he left as it was, wouldn't let anyone touch it; only the fountain he had put in working order. In one of the sheds he'd come across the fountain's old ornament, a little boy urinating, fashioned in stone, and this he had set up again. Guests are the only ones

---

* He attempts the English, rather than the Hungarian pronunciation of USA.
** Ödön Lechner (1845–1914). The best known architect of Hungarian art nouveau. His public buildings have made a lasting contribution to Budapest's cityscape.

nowadays who go into the garden occasionally. Eduárd gets about very little; his knees hurt. "When I was living over there, I used to travel ninety-six hours at a stretch; the trains' jolting put the cartilage out in my knees," he says, not the least bit interested in doctors. "And all for the sake of that cursed monarchy!" he adds mysteriously. "I pulled off big deals in heavy industry, they have a lot to thank me for." There's his little kitchen garden with two lines of red currant bushes and five peach trees at the end of the lawn. He has two horses, two milch cows, four pigs, a whole army of poultry; these are the proceeds. He had a tank built to collect rain, so that he could pipe in running water. The whole thing is such an expense, he can hardly afford guests and tobacco. But the driver of the Taksony bus had greeted me with the following: "Is it the castle you're wanting? I'll be stopping there!" It was homesickness brought Eduárd back and this question makes him happy. He even keeps two peacocks, perhaps because of that. He knows every bird personally, and keeps an eye on them all; each one even has a name. He suffered a heart attack once, and often speaks about it: "It was as if my heart had suddenly been put in a vice, even my ribs cracked. I was just looking down in front of me. Beautiful large fat globules were swimming in the golden-colored soup, and I had just taken hold of Lidi's thigh…" At this, guests who are not in on the joke exchange glances, and we burst out laughing. I knew this Lidi, a dark-brown noisy hen, one of Eduárd's favourites. To this day he guesses at a secret link between the hen's "transformation" and the heart attack.

We continue eating in reverential silence, except for Kormos who gives a snarl when finishing one bone and demanding another.

Eduárd bolts down a large bit of beef stewed with horse-radish onto which he ladles yet more horseradish, brushes away the tears with his fist, throws his fork down onto the table, and shouts at me:

"And I'm quite forgetting the most important thing of all! How is Fülöp?"

Startled by this sudden question, I take a sip of the wine and soda smoking ice-cold in front of me, and come out with it casually:

"He was elected to the Academy last week."

"Where?" Eduárd asks wide-eyed.

"To the French Academy," I reply impassively.

Mother clutches the table-napkin to her mouth, but the laughter dances in her eyes.

"I haven't read about it in the papers, although I would have if it were true," Eduárd says ominously. "Have you read it, by any chance?"

"I haven't read it, either," I reply nonchalantly, "because he's a futurist, the papers here didn't carry it, but they wrote to me from the Academy. They elected him to Victor Hugo's seat."

Mother fails to smother a titter. "I'll murder you!" storms Eduárd, lashing out; then he begins to laugh.

Fülöp is known to the entire family. Perhaps some three years ago, one Sunday after lunch I fell asleep in my deck chair in the garden. On the ground beside me lay a book of verse by Philippe Soupault. Eduárd strolled over, picked up the slim volume, and read it through. When I awoke around five o'clock, Eduárd was already giving a reading on the veranda, standing legs apart, the Petit Larousse on the table in front of him, Soupault's book in hand, translating the poems straight off; and around him were Béla, Uncle Miklós, the reverend from V., and Ferenc the carter. They were convulsed with laughter.

Docteur Breton va à Gien
par un temps de chien
Il est tombé dans un trou
*on ne sait où.**

He was just reading this, convulsed with laughter, when I got there.

"What is Victor Hugo compared to this," he announced triumphantly when he laid eyes on me. "This is the stuff to read, not Victor Hugo!"

* Doctor Breton goes to Trier
in quite awful weather.
Into a hole he did fall
unknown to all.

And since then Soupault has grown into a symbol. Eduárd labeled him a futurist and christened him Fülöp. And from time to time I used to receive postcards: once there was one of Notre-Dame in Paris, and on another occasion one of the Exchange in Brussels. "Taksony," the postmark proclaimed proudly. "Quite by accident I happened to read your Sunday poem. It could have been written by Fülöp. Embraces, Eduárd." Or: "I acknowledge receipt of your book parcel with thanks; half of the poems reveal Fülöp's profundities. Just keep it up, E."

And by this time Fülöp was known to everyone. Also to Uncle Mérges, the joiner from B., who now and again did repairs on the house under Eduárd's personal supervision to the accompaniment of continuous swearing in both English and Hungarian.

But we love each other, and the taunting always ends in great demonstrations of friendship. We savor the wine and I tell him about Paris; he blinks as he tells me about America. And in order to prove our theories, we both make up little stories with a twist to drive home the point. "You really are quite a storyteller, Eddie dear," mother observes more than once, while she does her crocheting beside us. To which Eduárd grunts: "Why not a poet and be done? All I'm telling you is the absolute truth!" Yet I smile to myself as I recognize among the American stories, now and again, one of Mikszáth's* anecdotes patched up and decked out in New York colors; but at times like these Eduárd is oblivious to my smile, the source having already sunk into his subconscious.

And in the overcast, pitch dark, resounding night he takes his cane, snatches up the coachman's lantern and with unsteady knees walks ahead of us, swinging the lamp as he conducts us to the bus stop. And when that ark rolls up, he gives me an affectionate rub with his beard. And they stand in the highway dust, mother and he, hand in hand looking after me.

I wait for the train in the sooty darkness of the station, my mind a blank, and suddenly there appears before me the

* Kálmán Mikszáth (1847–1910). Novelist, short-story writer, publicist. Greatest early figure of realistic prose and master of satiric, anecdotal representation.

illumination of a gesture, a gesture of mother's: we are shelling green peas in the garden, and before we start she puts on a pair of glasses. She had never worn them before. Time rings its bell when the dark little station begins to speak.

I make the journey back from childhood in the jolting, badly-lit carriage. My eyes keep falling shut, and when I look out my bristly face stares back at me from the window through which a few lights flicker.

And from one end of the open day-coach, through the sleep-inducing rattle, I hear a wakening voice, a woman's, persisting in its disbelief in French, on the Taksony–Áporka–Dömsöd line: "*Tu crois que c'est pour cela?*" And another woman's voice answering, in a somewhat self-assured tone: "*Je ne le crois pas, je le sais. Tout de même l'enfance c'est quelque chose!*"*

The train halts, and as people begin moving around I'm all ears. A brilliant yellow knitted coat disappears through the door as I glance up.

"They're getting off," I think, startled and curious about what will come next. I get my things together and jump off. Ferencváros railway station. I hurry toward the exit. The two voices have vanished, and so has the yellow coat.

"Childhood is a great thing." I say the sentence over, tormented by the feeling that I ought to be inspired to think of something important to say about it, but nothing comes to mind.

Of course, it was Jean. My anxiety dissipates. Jean had said it years earlier. And yesterday Jean arrived from Paris; we had dinner together; and afterwards at home I began to write about Ági.

"Childhood is a great thing," I smile now as I say it again nodding and applauding myself.

SATURDAY. We were not doing anything at the time. Just looking at books in the Odéon arcades or along the *quais* with bored yet dogged persistence. Casually working our way through them, we rummaged with grave gestures

---

* "Do you think, that's the reason?"
"I do not think, I know. All the same, childhood is a great thing!"

in the boxes, sometimes reading aloud to each other twenty lines of Racine or two or three snippets from the sermons of Bossuet. Sometimes for minutes on end, looking at a couple of boring engravings until, both our backs beginning to ache at the same time, we pressed our hands with an identical gesture into the small of the back. We gave a stretch and a groan.

Tired out, dusty hands swinging at our sides, we set off next for the Luxembourg. Jean Citadin did not utter a word, walking along beside me; he didn't trouble to close his mouth while whistling some children's song. After a while he broke off and just went on quietly sucking in air between his teeth. I threw him a look, for it was getting on my nerves.

"Well, are you still fond of Cocteau?" he asked, ready for battle.

Jean Citadin and I had become friends in a country town back home. He had gone there to visit a friend of his for three days and ended up spending two months—from sheer indolence. With sunburned face, he paced angrily along beside me. We were striding toward the outskirts of the city between bushy topped acacias.

"Cocteau's a conjurer," he explained, finger uplifted. Visible on the tip of his forefinger, as if some accented syllable had landed there, were the bushy acacia crowns. Alongside us dogs snapped through the fences, but he didn't even notice.

"Cocteau is a conjurer, and I don't like conjurers. They cheat. Cocteau cheats too. Behind all his show, there's nothing. Poets shouldn't be tricksters; poets should touch the heart. Like Villon, Ronsard, Verlaine!"

"That's the reader's attitude, but you are a poet! Your aesthetics are somewhat narrow, considering. Sentimental aesthetics!"

"No, I'm not a poet yet," he protested. "Language is still a problem; it puts obstacles in my way; it's malicious, obstinate. The poem still has the feel of having been worked on. There's still a great deal of showing off about it, of conjuring, trickery. As I say, I don't care for those who conjure. A poem should convey feeling like a whistle does, an exclamation, or a wino's hiccup. It shouldn't give the impression of being made of a particular substance! Is one aware of the stones of Strasbourg cathedral?"

39

It was around noon when we left, and the moon accompanied us home. Cocteau provided an excuse for a dispute, and we disputed endlessly.

Now he picked a quarrel. It was a long time since we'd argued, a long time since we had talked together. Lazy and hesitant, we sauntered through Paris, idling the days away aimlessly. Neither of us did a thing. Sometimes we slept for days, other times hardly at all for days on end.

We walked around the city, loitering in front of shop-windows, hanging around the *quais* reading the afternoons away at various book boxes, sitting in the squares playing with children and girls: many times the two of us with just one girl, many times with ten children.

"Well?" he asked.

"I like him," I said, as if to myself, "one day I'm even going to translate some of his poems into Hungarian."

"Keeping to the form!" Jean completed the sentence for me, emphasizing the last word ironically.

"That's right!" I'm raging inside, "but not the way you do, poems in prose! Mallarmé's a great artist when it comes to form, isn't he?" Suddenly, I prepare a trap.

"Certainly he is!" Jean walks into it unsuspectingly.

"Well, this great artist of form, this professional devotee of the English language translated Poe's 'Raven' into prose. And how do you think he renders the word, the one the raven utters continually, 'Nevermore'? *Jamais plus!* That's the meaning, isn't it? However, that's not enough by a long chalk! The English has about it a dark, shivering atmosphere and suggests something, conveys something of the sound of croaking! Surely that's why it has posed such a great problem for our poets. The greatest of the moderns have translated it faithfully according to the form, taking great pains over this particular word. One of them translated it like this, let your ear be judge, listen to this word: *Sohamár!*"

At once Jean's face lit up and, like someone who'd just hit on a solution, he whispered: "Tell me now, what does the raven say in your language?"

"*Kár,*" I answered, taken by surprise, "it says *kár,* and from this we get the verb *károg.*"

"Is that what it says?" Jean shook his head.

40

"That's it," I affirmed.

"Well, you see, that's not what the French raven says. It just says *Krrr Krrr*... Do you think, the English one says *More...More...*? So much for this sort of fidelity to form!"

I became angry, and stood confronting him.

"Now, look here. You know Tibullus's *Detestatio belli*, don't you? Book one, tenth elegy? The one which starts with: *Quis fuit, horrendo primus qui protulit enses?*"

"*Quam ferus et vere ferreus ille fuit!*"* With a laugh, Jean completed the quotation.

"Oh, I beg your pardon, I'm forgetting you're a Greek and Latin specialist," I said with irony. "Well, I translated it into Hungarian—in distichs, naturally, so as to be faithful to the form. Can't imagine it, can you? But this is not what's important; just listen: *divitis hoc vitium est auri, nec bella fuerunt*, the eighth or the tenth line, *faginus astabat cum scyphus ante dapes.*** Now here comes the Hungarian distich!

Mindez a sárarany átka, sosem volt háború addig,
 *míg kopogó fapohár járta a víg lakomán.****

"Not bad." Jean showed surprise.

"Not bad?" I stormed, "Excellent! And the pentameter's even more beautiful than in the Tibullus because it's clean, doesn't drag; this way, it gives greater atmosphere to the line. *'Míg kopogó fapo-hár jár-ta a víg lako-mán'!*"

"More beautiful than Tibullus?" Jean expressed amazement.

"Just this particular line," I said modestly, "surely you can hear!"

The line certainly made an impression on Jean. He had me repeat it; he said it after me and gave a whistle. But then he declared that something like this counts as individual creativity, not as translation, because it is not exact, not true.

"What's important is being faithful to the original," he raised a forefinger, "and that's why it's not possible to trans-

---

* What man, what devil, first conceived the sword?
  Shaper of iron, himself an iron heart!
** Actually, the seventh and eighth lines. The Hungarian text reads "*adstabat.*"
*** Gold taught us to kill our fellows. There were no wars when wooden cups stood
  at the simplest feast.

41

late according to the form. Fidelity to form! Give the line back its spondee, don't make it more beautiful; let it be true, if it's to be done at all... We do things precisely, we don't fool around with poems in other languages; we tell the truth about them in French."

"Truth? Without form? How can formless poems be true? The form is basic, old chap. That's what strikes to the heart. No embezzling of even one of the poem's alliterations. What's that? Impossible, you say? But that's what truth is. It's still possible to give back value equal to that of the original. You can make up in a later line what you may have missed in an earlier; then the poem's wholeness won't be any the worse! Will it make the poem any different? What's your difficulty? Some pet theory? It's for you to say!"

He was mumbling something to himself, and I saw that he was no longer interested in the difficulties of translation. The discussion had interested me, for at that period I'd begun to be acquainted with those secret and intimate pathways of French literature; virgin territory to alien promenaders, they quite conquered me. That's why I had to be somewhat disparaging, defensive... Resentful, I held my peace.

Jean was sucking in both cheeks between his back teeth, biting down. This is the way he walked beside me, with misshapen face, his head nodding. We came to the gardens. We kicked pebbles in front of us. Already the golden tones of the flagging afternoon settled among the trees; the children's monotonous, playful cries were a faint hum. We sat down beside the fountain. Sticking the toes of our shoes under the rungs of our seats, we tipped back and forth.

Jean was quiet, a forefinger propping up his nose. I gazed at the fish and at how much the water lily had opened up since yesterday. I told the time by it. "I'm growing older," I thought, and had a sudden feeling of hurrying. As if I were late for an appointment. But I knew I always felt this way when afternoon seeps away into evening, and stayed where I was.

"Interesting." Jean abruptly set the chair down flat beneath him. "An interesting association."

"What is?" I asked sulkily, pretending boredom.

"I liked to prop my nose up this way when I was a child too, often got my hand slapped for it."

I continued tipping back and forth, expectantly.

"It crossed my mind just now," he drawled on, "as if it were yesterday, I must have been eight or nine at the time. We were living on Vaugirard. Mother was still beautiful in those days; there was a pale blue birthmark just beneath one ear. It looked like a bite. I think men were tempted to nibble. Uncle Jacques used to come to our place, when father went to work at the office...

"Uncle Jacques was 'an acquaintance,' but father didn't like him. He often came at a time when father was at work. In his fifties, tall, white-haired, red-faced. He helped us, I know, I don't know in what way or why, and I don't much care. But I know we were grateful to Uncle Jacques. I partly loved him, yet partly hated him. Hated him, because he loved mother and didn't like father who didn't like him either. Yet loved him, because when he came it was always an event. Whenever he left there was always quarreling, and often my little sister Claire and I got a spanking; but when he came he always brought something. And it wasn't very often we got things. Poor father...

"That was the time I was furiously dashing off masses of sketches. Uncle Jacques always looked at them, and praised my drawing; he didn't alter them with ugly thick lines like my real uncle who's a painter. That's why I liked him. Drawing was very important to me then, because my brother Pierre was only four years older than I and yet already he was living away from home. He'd learned to draw, was living with uncle, having adventures, and bragging to me.

"Well, then, on the afternoon I'm talking about, Uncle Jacques brought me a sketchbook with a canvas cover. For Claire there was chocolate. Mother bundled us out into the other room. Claire made a fuss, for she didn't want to go. I didn't protest. Inside me stirred a small particle of hate, but it was repressed by happiness mixed with the gratitude I felt over the sketchbook. Claire sat snuffling on the floor, her tears of anger trickling down; her mouth full, she crammed the chocolate in noisily, desperately. I'd ask her for some, but I knew she wouldn't give me any. I took out a pencil and india rubber; leaning forward over the table, I began to draw a landscape with a castle on top of a hill. I wasn't satisfied with it; perhaps the sketchbook was too beautiful. I could hear them carefully turning the key in the door. I glanced at Claire, to see whether she'd heard it. She gave no sign. With drawn face she sat on the floor folding silver paper. I went on sketching for a while. With brutal suddenness, a door opened in there. We leapt up. The locked door was open, and we ran into the room. Behind the other door, mother and Uncle Jacques sprang apart."

Jean jerks the chair forward beneath him; his hands have ceased their gesturing. He turns away from me to watch the water. He feels me looking at him. Then shrugging his shoulders, he goes on in a bored tone:

"Mother was all red and dishevelled. Uncle Jacques was his usual pink self, but just then he was panting too. I was given a caress, also an 'apricot' pinch on the head. About that pinch, to this day I don't know who gets the pleasure: the one who gets or the one who gives? I certainly didn't. I was pretty well behaved as a child though. Uncle Jacques gave Claire a kiss, but Claire gave him back a kick on the leg. Mother smacked Claire on the head, Uncle Jacques laughed, and Claire started howling…"

"And then?" I turned towards Jean Citadin, who was staring before him, withdrawn into himself.

"What do you mean, then?"

"What happened next?"

"Nothing," he answered, standing up. We made our way toward the gate. We strode along slowly and with deliberation. The diluted twilight was fading fast.

"But now perhaps I understand," Jean murmured to himself.

"What?" I asked sharply, remembering that I felt hurt.

"Why," he answered with a mollifying gesture, "that before I met you this afternoon, Louise and I had a quarrel."

I was silent.

"I asked her to come up to my place. I'm tired, let's cut the cackle; I'm no Romeo. She didn't come. We had a quarrel. When we shook hands, this is what she said: 'The trouble is, Jean, that my mother never cheated on my father…' Understand?" he turned to me, screwing up his eyes.

"Naturally," I shrugged, "and you believe…"

44

"I don't believe, I know. Childhood's a great thing." Jean gave a whistle and glanced around with a marveling look on his face. Then he plunged a hand into his pocket, stuck a cigarette languidly in his mouth, and with the smoker's accomplice smile sought a light from an old man gawking around him at the gardens' entrance gate.

TUESDAY. "I can taste childhood on my tongue," Jean said one night in Paris, "I taste its flavors whenever I'm suddenly reminded of it. Often, it comes to mind from certain flavors too. And sometime," he added shyly, "from the smell some women have."

"With me, it's sounds," I answered, "sometimes only rustlings, melodies too sometimes, then often whole dialogues will start inside me. And if I hear someone... has died... death always makes me think of it..."

I get up, drink a glass of water, and go out onto the balcony. During the night the wind had half-pulled up a white petunia, and I smooth it back into the soil again, wash my hands, escape... But then I sit down at the table again, and listen. And I hear the buzzing of flies, clouds of flies beating the air around me. I concentrate, and the buzzing grows faint, small bare feet go clap-clap on the earth, and I see—though, in reality, at the time I did not—many tiny flames rise, flickering, from the tracks in the dust. Dust. Slithering soles beneath the window scuff out a track. I am waving a large piece of a branch from a walnut tree, chasing away flies from father's face. Without turning my head, I can feel them peeping through the crack in the curtain. Pista and Feri are waiting for me, wanting to play.

And again I hear the flies.

Voices filter through the buzzing, no more than a breath: my name. They're calling me. Though I do not move, I'm listening intently. Two flies have settled on father's sweating face; they start to crawl around, and fly off when I move the branch. Again they're calling. I brace my heels on the floor, and stiffen my back. I have to stay here, father's ill, and the flies won't let him sleep. "Always playing, that's all they do!" I fume.

"Go on out... play." Then I hear father's hoarse, tired

voice; startled, I swing the branch toward him. While I'd stopped watching, the flies had awakened him. I keep moving the branch, looking at father lying there with eyes closed. I do not answer.

"Go on out, son," he says quietly, without opening his eyes.

"I don't want to," I answer quickly, slightly offended.

"They're calling you out to play, don't you hear?"

"They're not really calling." I trace a pattern with the toe of my shoe.

Again the voice whispers, more insistently. Father has gone back to sleep. There's a round-headed shadow cast on the curtain, Feri with his close-cropped head. He raises an arm, extends it, inclines his head as he takes aim, clenches his hand into a fist, and goes click with his forefinger: *pow!* The shadow trembles blackly in front of the window. "They're calling me out to play cops and robbers." It starts to get to me. I keep moving the branch, without answering, and the shadow suddenly runs away from the window. Right afterwards in a flash there's another thrown on the curtain, Pista.

I go on waving the branch. Sometimes the flies stick together, buzzing: I snatch at them with my free hand.

Carefully, the door is pushed open and gives out a long sigh. On the threshold stands Uncle Miklós, mother's brother-in-law, at whose place we are living. He mops his brow and leans against the doorjamb, which gives a loud crack.

"Shhh..." I rebuke him, with self-important reproach.

He registers alarm and jerks his chin in my direction questioningly. I shrug my shoulders. He averts his face and goes out on tiptoe again, leaving the door ajar. I slide halfway down in my chair so that I'm balancing on the edge, not knowing what I should do. If I go as far as the door the flies will wake father up; if I leave it open, kitchen sounds will be heard inside and the noise will wake him.

Mother enters, with Aunt Margit. They come in without a sound and, standing at the foot of the bed, stare at father in silence. Quite some time passes like this; then mother beckons to me and starts toward the door. I follow her, while Aunt Margit takes the branch from my hand, settles herself down in the chair, and begins fanning father. In the kitchen, mother sits on a stool and pulls me toward her; pressing me between her knees, she takes hold of my elbows.

"You're not a child anymore now. You're eleven years old, a big boy, aren't you?" I nod seriously, in the manner appropriate at such times.

"Your father's very ill. The local doctor doesn't know what is the matter; he says we should take him back home to Pest. To the hospital. What do you think?..."

"Let's take him home," I say, touched by the voice seeking advice.

"Yes, of course, that's what I think; but how can we do it? Uncle Miklós has so much work piling up on him here, Aunt Margit's making preserves. I can't leave father and Ági here... You can't take him along either, and we can't put him on the train or in a cart. You know what I thought? You'll make the journey to Pest, and go to Uncle Kari's on Hadnagy Street. Then you'll tell them what's happening here, that Kari should arrange for a car, and bring a doctor along with him from Pest. Alright?"

"Alright, I'll go then." I want to move, but mother holds me firmly between her knees.

"Listen to me just a little longer. You can't go now, the noon train has already left, and there isn't another until late evening. There's more I want to say about it. You know, the station's an hour and a half from here. You'll go along the highway; you'll leave good and early, no need to run. It'll be evening and dark by then, but you won't be afraid, will you? A Winnetou is never afraid! You know, Juci the sow may have her piglets at any moment, so no one can go with you. Aren't you tired? Don't you want to go and have a little lie down? Or would you rather go and play? Off with you then!"

She gives me a playful pat on the back and walks toward the room. I take a few steps after her, wanting to say that I won't be afraid on the road, but mother's already opening the door.

"This poor man's going to die, you know." I hear Aunt Margit's voice. In a daze, I stagger out into the yard and sit down on the wood-chopping stump; between my nails I pick up the tiny splinters of wood that lie all around and collect them in my palm. I sit there till evening, when they call me to dinner.

I'm so tired that my eyelids fall shut as I stand in the doorway while rain pours down. Mother pulls the hood of my coat down over my brow, reties my shoelaces, and buttons the flap of my pocket containing the fare money. Aunt Margit stuffs an apple into my coat. "I don't want it," I say, "it makes a bulge." "Just take it along, it'll be good on the train," mother says, encouragingly. She turns me around, looking me over once again from all sides. "Well, off you go. Give Ági a kiss, then you may leave. She's inside with father."

I tiptoe in. The lamp is smoking, and Ági is sitting in the chair shooing away the flies. When she sets eyes on me, the corners of her mouth droop, as they always do before she cries, and tears collect along her eyelids. She plants a wet kiss on my nose; I kiss her back, stroking her hair like the grown-ups do. I look toward the bed. Father is sleeping; the bones of his face are sharp, his blond beard sticks straight out, and his forehead glistens with perspiration. "Father," I call, quietly. "Don't you see? He's sleeping!" Ági snuffles. I chase a fly off of the blanket and go out. There's the smell of Uncle Miklós's wine-laden breath, Aunt Margit's cooked vegetable dish, and for a long time, mother's nice scented soap lingering. The two of us go hand in hand out into the rain; mother accompanies me along the street, a shawl over her shoulders.

"Go on back, you're going to get wet," I say; but she accompanies me as far as the crucifix where the highway begins. She clutches me to her; then turning back, she starts to run. The shawl is flapping, it's as if an angel were running; soon only the white shawl is visible, the shawl running alone through the air, ghostly, disembodied. I turn away, frightened, and begin to pick my way through the mud. The apple presses into me; I take it out from my pocket, and bite into it. The wind springs up, slashing rain across my face and into my mouth; my nose is stuffed up with chewed apple and tears, and I feel my heart swelling. I want to throw the apple away, but instead just quietly let it drop in the mud. Taking small steps I walk along the deserted, glistening dark road; I try to pull myself together, and I'm afraid.

I can hear the rain drumming amid the rustling and creeking of the trees. I hear footsteps and begin to run; behind me the steps run too. I stop; the steps are heard no more. I run on, glancing back again and again. A bicycle is coming toward me, its lamp wobbling through the dark; I cower over to the side by the ditch, and stop. "It could be a murderer," I shiver. The bicycle splashes mud to either side; the man on it half-stands as he peddles, swearing and hissing between his teeth. He doesn't notice me. I start off again, my shoes becoming slippery inside with the wet, my shirt plastered to my neck. The trees step out in front of me mutely, with frightening stamping motions, without a sound, continually blocking my way; I almost have to push them aside in order to go on. Again and again I glance over my shoulder. White shadows flutter behind me like those upon the window at home at night sometimes, thin, swaying heads bending now to right, now to left. Before the station, a dog rushes out from the Ferenczi farmhouse with a howl and springs at me; his legs go stiff with fright as he tries to stop, but the momentum carries him right up to my shoes. With a low scream I kick out at him; he skids on his tail with a yelp, a snap, and we side-step round each other, petrified. I can make out only his teeth and the whites of his eyes. One shouldn't run, I know; slowly I back away. He follows for a little while with his sharp barking, then with large bounds suddenly disappears.

I put down my pen, heart pounding as if I'd been running, like someone who has escaped from danger, I lay my head on my arms. From the desk I hear sighing; it's a humid wind blowing through foliage. Is it the wood remembering the time when it was alive? I lean forward across it, palms down, until the boards seem to become rounded!

And beyond the curtain of rain I see the station lamp, disappearing and blinking out again. Is the wind turning it? A new worry nags me. I'll have to buy a ticket. As I push open the station door, water pours down my neck. I knock against a table in the dark. A lamp comes on at the noise, and a voice asks, "What is it?" I go toward the light and stop in front of the little window. "What do you want?" A man in shirtsleeves rubs his fist across his eyes. "A ticket, to Pest."

"There's another thirty minutes," he mutters. He struggles to his feet from a small bench, puts on his coat, sits down in an officious manner at the small table, tears off something, stamps it, and slaps the money down on the table. "Well, sit down then, there'll be a signal when it comes."

I am sitting in the darkness, and it's only now that father comes into my mind again. I hear Aunt Margit's voice; is he really going to die? And I don't understand. But I pull my stomach in and slump forward. It must be serious for them to be sending me to Pest like this, at night, and all by myself. And if I die during the journey, or robbers derail the train, what then? And if Uncle Kari doesn't get the message? Uncle Miklós wouldn't be as likely to die by some mischance as I might; and if he were traveling, the train wouldn't get derailed either. He really could have come, despite Juci the pig. And all of a sudden, drowsiness overtakes me, and I feel at peace, proud too.

"They've trusted me to do it," I'm thinking, and my head falls forward.

The bell rouses me; then with the smell of soaked clothing in my nostrils, I drop off again. I found myself seated between two huge skirts; heat radiates upon me from two enormous market women. I'm being covered by their wet stiff skirts. I'm slipping down further; darkness falls upon me.

I am sitting in the dusky room, large shadows fly from the shelves, the faraway twilit hill looms in my window. On the pharmacy opposite, the glare of an illuminated sign shines up, throws flickering red onto the ceiling. What else do I remember?—with a shiver I look at the paper glimmering in front of me. I was standing in front of the East Station, still half-asleep, streetcars were gliding through the slow morning twilight and dark veils fluttered in the air. A key turns in the lock, and Fanni enters quietly. I feel her kiss on my forehead; she moves to and fro in the room with faint sounds, her skirt rustling. She turns on the light above the armchair.

"That was the time father died, you know," I say on impulse. "I know," she breathes gently; she shows no surprise. "Tell me this then, how did I get from the East Station up to Hadnagy Street?" "I don't know, my dear." She sets the table for dinner.

And then I rang the doorbell; it was an old house with a high door, and I had to stretch up to reach the bell. I waited for a while, then rang again. Uncle Kari stood tall in the doorway, clutching his long nightgown close about his neck. Beside him in a nightdress, stood Aunt Hilda, a Prussian, even taller than my uncle. "What's happened, for God's sake? How did you get here?" my uncle called down to me. "Mother sent me to have you arrange for a car and a doctor because father's going to die!" "*Was sagt er?*" asked the aunt. Both at the same time, they squatted down beside me on the threshold.

"And do you know, we weren't even present there at the funeral, Ági and I?" I said during dinner. After a few days, mother took me away from Uncle Kari's to a lady's, an acpuaintance with whom Ági was already staying. Mother slept there too, coming back in the evenings. "Father's very ill, he can't even have visitors," mother would say, each evening crying as she said it. She wore a white dress, though the tears ran down her face. At first when this happened we were quiet; but then somehow we got used to father being very ill and mother crying and her seeing us only in the evenings. Besides, at the lady's we were given masses of cakes, and were getting out of hand. And no longer heeding even mother, we went chasing each other round the room, shrieking and knocking over chairs. And then one evening mother suddenly called us to her; Ági sitting on one knee and I on the other, she looked at us and again burst out sobbing. That's when she told us father had died, right after they brought him to Pest. Ági and I gazed at mother who was crying wildly; we understood nothing of the whole business, but mother kept on sobbing and clutching us to herself. We flung ourselves upon her and began to cry, too. Next day mother left in the early morning, and returned

51

with a black dress and black veil. She put a black dress on Ági; she'd also brought two black ribbons, one she tied in Ági's hair, the other she sewed on my right sleeve. We stood there quietly while she spoke to the lady, then she took us by the hand. And we set out to visit father in the cemetery.

FRIDAY. *All for nothing, oh for nothing!*
Father's dead. In turn they all have died.
Yet all of those who once did live with me
live on today too in my heavy heart;
and one light vibration is sufficient —
if across my hand a butterfly should flutter,
or a branch brush against my shoulder —
they give a sign, whose bodies are by now
an intimate smile, perfume, or flower,
only their bones lie cramped up underground. *

Father died two months ago.
I'm lying in my aunt's bed, a high darkish-brown old woman's bed; fleshy-soft bed-linen imprisons me within its warmth. This bed is like a big old ship, deep and creaky, around which white clouds swim. Sometimes it rocks. I've got jaundice, and they brought me here in a hackney cab three days ago. When they took me away, Ági cried and mother argued with Uncle Lajos. It was about her being quite able to look after me too, the aunt's not needed. She'll make me well, just lend her some money. She even knows a doctor, a real cheap one. And when I sat up on the sofa and cried out protesting that I didn't want to go away, that I didn't want it either, then mother started to cry. They still took me away though, because Uncle Mihály the guardian wanted it. This

* Péntek. Hiába minden, ó hiába!
Meghalt apa. S meghaltak sorra mind.
De mindazok, akik csak vélem éltek,
élnek ma is nehéz szívemben és
elég egy könnyű rebbenés,
kezemre hogyha röpke lepke száll,
vagy ág érinti vállamat,
Ők adnak jelt, akiknek teste már
meghitt mosolygás, illat vagy virág
s csak csontjaik szorongnak lenn a föld alatt.

distant, mysterious uncle was my guardian, though I didn't understand what a guardian was. It can't be anything bad, because Ági has mother as guardian. But why isn't she mine too? Why must a brother and sister have two guardians?

I have been here at the aunt's for three days. I've got jaundice, a lovely mysterious illness; no one in my class has ever had it, and it doesn't hurt. My aunt has the collected works of Jókai; she's promised me the sort of cake which is all filling; she's given me the Poets' Album, and says that when I'm big she'll give me the Jókai too. I've got three pencils, and my school books have stayed home.

It's good being ill this way. The bed feels good; I tumble about, and I know that something is going on around me. The family is growing: many new relatives come and go, even ones whose names I've never heard before, all bringing small presents, all hiding something. I can smell their indulgence and their surprise. Somehow I've become important; they tempt me, and everything's more and more mysterious. I make ever newer experiments, experiments that succeed. The Frommer pistol is the only thing I haven't got yet, though I've been demanding it for a long time, having discovered it in a drawer even before coming to live here. Beside the stove my aunt sits sewing; turning toward her I address her sternly from the bed:

"Aunt, give me the Frommer!"

I'd been quiet a long time, and she thought I had fallen asleep. She gives a start and shakes her head.

"In that case, I'm going home!" I haven't the slightest intention of going; I'm enjoying myself; I don't want to go anywhere, I just want to blackmail her. Her feeble protestations encourage me. I repeat the syllables louder and louder, then shout out the two sentences; my aunt steadily shakes her head after each demand, thus goading me on to roar out my threat again and again. My aunt's refusal is no longer needed; the two sentences run together with no meaningful pause; by now they've lost their meaning, long since obliterated in the senseless repetition; only the sound is important now, the noise I'm making. My howls fill the room, I'm becoming heated, sweating with the strain, driven on by knowledge of my power. While the shouting's going on, the

53

door to the next room opens and Uncle Lajos comes in. He halts and looks at me thoughtfully. Suddenly I feel tired, and I stop.

Uncle Lajos pulls up a chair to my bedside and sits down. My aunt goes out. Not a word passes between them, but I can see they've agreed on something; I sense something solemn in the way they move. After the shouting I can actually feel silence swishing past, its coolness fanning my ears, and I begin sinking downwards along with the bed. Suddenly, darkness and clammy cold envelop me, and I am listening intently as if from within a deep well. From high up, my uncle begins to speak:

"So, you want to go home!"

"Yes!" I answer, with feeble stubbornness, without conviction. All at once, meaningless fear rises inside me. The bed begins to rise along with my voice, returning to its old place beside him.

"You are at home now, here," he answers, and glances at the ceiling. "Where else could you go to?"

"Home. To mother and Ági."

"To mother, to mother..." Silence, he doesn't look at me, he's looking sideways. "To your stepmother!" he says, after a long pause, forcing out the word from deep inside him. Relieved that he could come out with it, he gets to his feet and begins to pace the room. I sit up in bed; my throat is swollen, and I choke back a sob with my anger. "It's not true!" I flare up and I want to shout.

"Yes, yes, stepmother," comes the response. Fear seizes me, stifling my protest. I can sense the agitation behind the quiet voice; his pacing quickens, and I follow him with my eyes.

"You're a big boy now, you should know. She's a good woman, you should love her; she has brought you up for the past ten years, been a mother to you in place of your mother, but..."

"It's not true!"

"But it is, son. Your mother, your real mother died when you were born. You were one year old when your poor father married your mother."

"You're lying!"

54

He sits down again on the chair beside my bed and looks at me. His voice is tired and affectionate.

"Why should I lie, little chap? That's how it was! And your mother's very poor, she can't bring up two children. She doesn't want this, she says she can work to support you as well; but that would be very hard. Tell her you'll stay here!"

"I won't stay!"

"My dear, dear boy, why make your mother's lot more difficult!"

"But it's not true that mother's not my mother!"

"Anna!" He calls toward the adjoining room, and abruptly gets to his feet. My aunt enters, pale and apprehensive. "His temperature will go up again," she says, averting her eyes from me. "Where's the picture?" my uncle asks with an awkward gesture, and stamps his foot.

I am sitting up in bed, there's a sharp pain in my eyes; I'm shivering, and I know that it's true. Once, a long time ago, with mother we went into a shop for something; the shopkeeper greeted her as an acquaintance and enquired after relatives. Ági and I both said our names; and when asking about me, the shopkeeper said: "You did get the boy, then?"

"Get him? I bore him, my good man!" And she threw her arms around me. I looked up at mother and saw her put her finger to her lips and shake her head angrily. They talked for some time, and when we left I turned on her:

"Why did that man say you had got me?"

"The nice man had mixed you up with someone else."

"Who with? Who's the one who was got, then?"

"Did you get me too?" asked Ági's tiny frightened voice. Mother became angry.

"I didn't get anyone! Don't be silly. The gentleman mixed you up with the Fazekas family. They got a child once."

"Who are the Fazekases?" I can hear my voice, and the child got and the one born became mixed up inside me, because the one who is born is also got. At first, each child is swimming in a great sea. But the got child is Ági, because mother got her once from God; I can even remember it. She got her in the clinic in Bakács Square. Father bought flowers for me, and I had to give them to mother when we visited her.

"The Fazekases don't even exist," I shiver, "We're the Fazekases... I'm the got child!"

Aunt comes in, pats a little hollow in the blanket and sets a picture in front of me. "Here's your mother. You see, I didn't lie!" my uncle murmurs.

I look at the picture. A beautiful serious woman, a stranger to me, is standing in the picture; she has on a hat with white roses, a white dress with flounces, and is looking to one side thoughtfully. I just stare without touching it.

Aunt approaches the bed and lays the Frommer beside the picture. Slowly, I put out a hand from under the blanket. I raise the pistol, cradle it against my cheek; closing an eye, I take aim at the catch on the window.

My aunt lets out a sharp cry. I put the pistol down, and lie back.

My mind's gone blank; I'm feeling lonely and full of shivers. Then the first stirrings of a word within me, one I heard in an office a few days ago where we went with mother; a man with a beard said it of me because my father was dead. But that's not why he said it!

"I'm really orphaned now!" I shout, throwing myself back in bed, face to the wall, and begin to sob with my mouth open. I curl up, with pain in my knees, and a throbbing ache in my ears. The pillow grows wet; I slide down still further under the blanket. The pillow's corner is beside my mouth; I bite it, tear at it. My head is spinning.

When I awake, the room is empty. The windows gleam in the semi-darkness. I'm feeling weary and somehow a stranger to myself. "Anyway, I'm going to die," I'm thinking, "then they'll get a fright here..." Within me revenge rears its head; I'd like to punish everyone for everything. I fold my arms behind my back like I used to in school. I'm waiting for death.

Mother hurries along the passageway in front of the windows, her mourning veil flutters behind. She rings. Aunt enters the room and puts on the light. She snatches up the picture which has slipped down to the edge of the bed, the Frommer also, throws them into a drawer, and runs to open the door.

"How is the child?" I hear mother's voice; then she bursts in, kisses me on the forehead and feels my hand. She brings in coolness and has a nice smell.

"I kiss your hand!" That's how I greet her. At my voice she flinches, leans over me and looks into my eyes. "Give me a real kiss," she says, stroking my face with hers. I kiss her. Straightening up suddenly, eyes flashing, she says to my aunt sharply:

"Who told him? Who dared tell him? You?"

"Lajos did," my aunt breathes, frightened, backing toward the door.

"Curse him!" hisses mother. She lets her arms fall and stands staring in front of her wearily, helplessly. Then she sits on the edge of the bed, and tears begin trickling slowly from her eyes. I stroke her arm, and she nestles against my breast; sobs shake her. I want to cry too, but I can't. I put a hand on her head; I'd like to console her. "I ought to help somehow," I think, feeling old and wise. "Anyway, I'm going to die," I'd like to say, but don't dare. We are alone in the room among the then strange furniture and strange things.

Mother struggles to her feet, sits on the chair, dries her eyes, and smooths aside hair falling over her forehead.

"But Ági's still my sister?" I ask.

She nods, catching her handkerchief to her mouth, and sobs into it again.

And I was to live for a long time among the then strange furniture and strange things, while the furniture from our home wandered to N. with mother and Ági. And if I went there once or twice for a holiday every two or three years, I had to make friends with the old furnishings all over again.

"How did my mother die?" I asked my aunt, in the twilight, some three years later.

"Get on with your reading, and don't be asking silly things! She died!"

"Died how? And why did she die?" My voice must have made her frightened, because she turned to face me and clasped her hands.

"It was too much for her heart, it was a twin-birth."

"A twin-birth?" I said it over after her, amazed. "How many more things are people still hiding!" I ground my teeth together, and my hand flew into a fist. "What a family! Everything turns out differently than with other people, normal people!"

"Where's my twin now?" suspiciously, I pressed my aunt further.

"He died, he was sickly, he lived only a minute or two. He was a boy, too."

"And?"

"And what?"

"And... and did mother die because she had twins?"

"That she did"—my aunt quickly wiped away a tear. "Anyway, there's no helping it now, don't be asking; and besides, it's not fitting to speak of things like this. You should be ashamed!"

"But there's nothing not fitting about it!" I stormed. "And father?"

"Can't you leave me in peace? Your father wasn't in Pest; he only got there an hour later. Do your reading and leave me in peace!"

I take a deep breath, swallowing my heart back down.

"Only twenty-eight she was at the time, poor Ilona," my aunt cried suddenly, and went out to the kitchen. I pushed open the door after her, but she shut it again and turned the key from the kitchen side. "Do your homework, and leave me in peace," she shouted, her voice hoarse.

"If I'd been father, I'd have bashed that brat against the wall, you know that?" I shouted through the door.

"Are you crazy? What brat?" The door opened suddenly.

"Me," I hissed through clenched teeth, "for him, everyone died; only I am left! And no one'll ever know whether it was I or my brother who died. With twins, how can people tell?"

"Have you gone crazy?" the aunt's tears ceased. "Come on, we'll go to the cinema!"

"I'm not going to the cinema!" I raged. "Mother shouldn't have been allowed to have children; who was the stupid doctor who let it happen? I'll kill him!" I aimed a kick at a corner of the sofa, and rushed out into the street.

And then the beginning of something about which only poems can be written... would that be when youth began?

What years they were! Was it you who remained? Or the other? "You killed them," the voice was saying, "you killed them, you kill-ed th-em, you kill-ed th..."

AFTER MIDNIGHT. Father died, and mother died too. *Mother* lives far away, and Ági lives far away too. And one by one all the others have died; that America-goer, bullying dear Eduárd has just died too. Jean departed the day before yesterday. Once again, wing-spread news of mobilization; and up he went to the embassy. "May I have your service papers?" The clerk extended two fingers. Jean dug them out. The fellow scanned them, then returned them. "You'll travel back immediately; not to Paris though, but to your service depot. Have a good journey." He stuck out a hand. I was waiting in the street in front of the embassy. Jean was pale as he came out, and he told me all about it. I stopped a taxi. We went to the hotel, and from there to the station. We did not speak. And when he had to get on the train, we suddenly kissed each other. Today, he's already on the Maginot Line. And who knows whether I'm living? Whether he's living?

When does childhood end? And when does youth? And life? No one ever notices.

I could catch the moment only twice: when the petal left its place, and when it spun to the ground. And both of the flowers were tulips, and both of them were white.

And is the twirling petal already dead
beginning its descent?
*or does it die only on reaching earth?**

End of August 1939

* S halott-e már a perdülő szirom,
  ha hullni kezd?
  vagy akkor hal meg, hogyha földet ér?

SELECTED
POETRY

FEDERICO GARCÍA LORCA*

Because you were loved by Hispania
and lovers recited your poetry—
they could do nothing else when they came,
but kill you—for you were a poet.
The people fight their battle now without you,
Ai, Federico García!

1937

* Federico García Lorca (1898–1936), poet and dramatist, one of
the most important figures in modern Spanish literature. He was
shot by rebels shortly after the outbreak of the Spanish civil war.

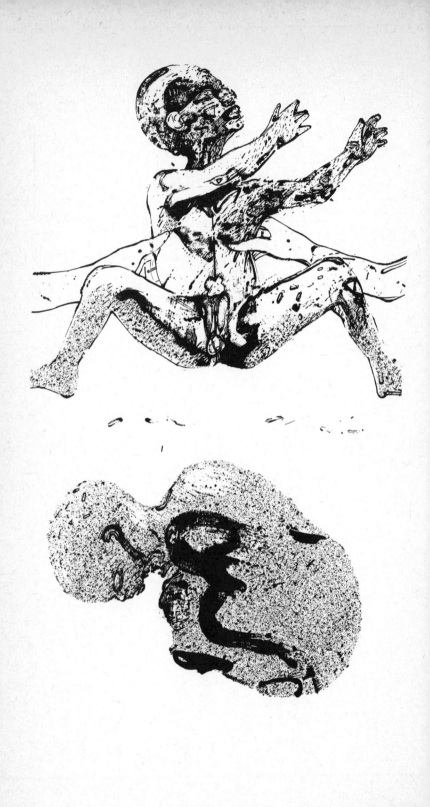

TWENTY-EIGHT YEARS

What an ugly, aggressive child I was—
your killer! my Mama of twins.
I don't know if you bore my younger brother
dead, or if he lasted five minutes,
but it's there, messy with blood, and wailing,
I was held to the light as a rather
triumphant little savage giving good
proof of his nature:
behind, two dead.

Behind me two dead,
the world all before,
from the same ditch sprung
as brigands;
orphaned I've sprung
out of this ditch
towards tough, strident
freedom's wide and windy roofs.

How despondent childhood was,
and how cold.
Your voice never calling,
it was a snake hissing at me
along my toy's track, blood sown
on my pillow at night—
to a child how appalling—
instead of big flakes of snowy down.

How despondent childhood was,
and how grand a youth!
Was it worth two dead?
I cried out to the portrait
blazing on my room's wall there.
You were twenty-eight *then*,
all of twenty-five there: a sincere
young woman, looking pensive,
contemplative.

You were twenty-eight *then,*
and that's the age I am today,
twenty-eight years you've been dead,
Mama! you gory runaway!

Mama, gory sacrifice,
I've reached my manhood,
the sun's on fire, I'm blinded,
show me that all this is good
by waving your gossamer hand, that you know,
and that I'm living my life as I should.

1937

GUARD AND DEFEND ME

The wind blowing at night through my dreams
and snowwhite sails flashing
slatting swelling and set for voyage far away.

I'm writing this slow poem here
like the emigrant starting his new life
and writing his poems from now on with a stick
in the shifting sands of far off Africa.

But from everywhere, from Africa too,
some ghastly crying can be heard,
the monstrous infant sucking day and night
at the purpled tits, by these times being nursed.

Of what worth's the word between two wars,
and what am I worth, a specialist
in words both difficult and rare, when every jerk's
stupidly clutching a bomb in his fist!

Flame's leaping across our skies and the reader
of signs in celestial lights hits the ground,
encircled by the whiteness of pain,
like the sea at ebb, with salt all around.

Guard and defend me, white pain,
and you, my snowwhite consciousness, stay with me here,
so that my clear word may never be fouled
by the brown smoke of burning fear.

1937

PEACE, HORROR

As I stepped out the door it was ten o'clock,
a baker singing glided by on glinting wheels,
a plane droned overhead, the sun shining, ten o'clock,
my dead aunt came to mind and suddenly on wings
all those I'd loved, none of them among the living,
a host of the mute dead all floating dark
and then some shadow slithering down the building's wall.
Silence dropped, morning was suspended at ten o'clock,
peace wafted through the street, and also horror's pall.

1938

FIRST ECLOGUE

Quippe ubi fas versum atque nefas: tot bella per orbem,
*tam multae scelerum facies;...**

Virgil

SHEPHERD
Been some time since I've seen you here. Thrush song's brought
you back at last?

POET
The wood's full of sounds. I can hear them. Spring's come!

SHEPHERD
Not yet. The sky's just teasing. Take a look at that puddle:
now it's dimpling; but when the freeze locks it up tonight
it'll snarl at you! Because it's April—damn fool's not to be trusted.
Those little tulips there are frost-burned.
Why so glum? Have a seat on this rock?

POET
Not that sad, actually. Just so used to this terrible world,
it sometimes can't even hurt anymore. Sickened, in fact.

SHEPHERD
I know. The blistered cannons on the peaks of the Pyrenees
are chatting among corpses frozen in their own blood,
bears and soldiers deserting the place together,
and regiments of women and kids and old folks with knotted
bundles running,
flattening themselves to the ground when death rolls overhead, and
there are too many bodies to bury.
I think you know Federico. Did he get away?

* The quotation is from Virgil's *Georgics:* "For here are right and wrong inverted;
so many wars overrun the world, so many are the shapes of sin..." (*Virgil*, trans.
H. Rushton Fairclough, Loeb Classical Library, London, 1930, 1 : 115).

POET

No. Murdered in Granada two years ago.

SHEPHERD

Lorca dead! Why wasn't I told?
Runners carrying rumor of war everywhere, yet the poet
disappears just like that! So—Europe mourns him not at all?

POET

Not even remarked. At best, the wind poking the embers
finds some broken lines in the pyre's stain, and notes them.
That's all curious posterity gets of the work.

SHEPHERD

Didn't get away. Died. Well, where could a poet run to?
Our own Attila* never made it either; just waved his hand,
always No to the Status Quo—but who's grieving over his
destruction?
And how are you doing? Can anyone hear you nowadays?

POET

Through the barrage? In these smoking shells of deserted villages?
I write anyhow, living at the heart of this insanity
like that oak tree: it knows it'll be cut down, and though
that cross blazed on its trunk bleaches and says the ax
clears this ground tomorrow, it puts new leaves out just the same.
You're all right; it's tranquil here; only the occasional wolf;
and you tend to forget you're keeping someone else's flock,
because it's months since the master's even been around.
So long now. It'll be deep night when I reach home:
the moth's already flitting, oozing silver from its wings.

1938

---

* Attila József (1905–1937). Poet and translator. One of the most important lyric
poets of twentieth-century Hungarian literature. He committed suicide by jump-
ing in front of a freight train.

THURSDAY

In New York, T* hung a halter
round his neck in some place he was rooming,
stateless through all those years, a drifter,
how much longer could he go on roaming?

In Prague, JM* took his life,
in his own land left with no homestead,
not one word a year does PR* write,
dead maybe under a root that's dead.

To Hispania he went, the poet,
where sorrow struck his eyes like a mist;
wanting to be free, and a poet,
could he cry against the bright dagger's thrust?

Could he cry to the infinite
when his finite journey is done;
could he cry out for his life,
the one in chains, or the homeless one?

When the lamb begins to bite
and the cooing dove eats bloody meat,
when the snake on the path whistles
and the blowing wind begins to scream.

26 May 1939

* "T" is Ernst Toller, a German playwright (1893–1939), who
committed suicide in Manhattan; "JM" is Jiři Mahen, pen-name
of Antonin Vančura (1882–1939), a Czech journalist and critic,
who killed himself not in Prague but in Brno; "PR" is Pierre
Robin, Radnóti's French poet friend who survived the war.

FOAMING SKY

The moon's rocked by a foaming sky,
miraculously I'm still living.
Hardworking death hunts this time
and those he comes across are livid.

Sometimes the year looks round and screams,
looks round, and then faints.
Behind me what an autumn skulks
and what a winter, blunt as sorrow's pain!

The forest bled and in the turning
time each hour's blood dribbled.
Great numbers and grim ones
that the wind on the snow scribbled.

I've lived to witness both this and that,
I feel the air as dense
as before I was born—that tepid
menacing silence is what I sense.

I stop here at the foot of the tree,
which roars its foliage furiously.
A branch snakes down. To throttle me?
I'm neither weak nor cowardly,

just tired. I stand still. And the branch, scared,
fumbles dumbly at my hair.
One ought to forget, but I've never
forgotten anything whatever.

Foam rages over the moon, anger
strikes a dark green streak across the sky.
Slowly, carefully, I roll myself
a cigarette. I'm alive.

8 June 1940

FOR A COPY OF *STEEP PATH**

This is one poet they don't seem to need,
though I merely mumble wordlessly;
◡—◡—◡— who cares—Satan's breed
can croon for you, not me.

And believe me, believe you me,
I suffer from that scared suspicion too!
One poet for whom the stake is only right,
because the truth is what I witness to.

The one who knows that snow is white,
that blood is red, the poppy's red.
And green the hairy poppy's stem.

This is the one whose death is decreed,
because he's never killed for them.

1 June 1939

---

* *Steep Path: Meredek út,* a collection
of Radnóti's poems, first published in 1938.

MY MEMORIES

Flowers pacing through my memories again...
I'm loitering beneath gusts of rain,
two women with bright, moist teeth approaching,
     then two pigeons. Their rotund
ostentatious bellies swag down along the ground.

That was a year ago. A drizzly, mild
dusk going to Senlis, and for a while
I was somehow oddly happy again;
     around me green walls stood
in silence, swaying, ferns filling those woods

and from Ermenonville that grove of young birch
trees, like some backward child coming at a lurch
towards us in her white skirt and a soldier
     round the bend standing in the glow
of the muddy, pleated earth. In his teeth a rose.

As if through the sky some brilliance fleeted...
Facing me Gyula* and Susan* are seated,
next to me Fanni, in whose eyes the landscape
     flows past, and overhead it seems
as though the gay mane of our railroad car streams

---

* Gyula and Susan: the Ortutays, who accompanied the Radnótis to
Paris. Gyula Ortutay (1910–1978) was one of the greatest Hungarian
ethnologists of the century.

and dearest Paris awaiting us by nighttime.
Nonstop death's roared through there too meantime,
and collected his colorful bouquet,
      Hectic and bloodstained, the copse
of birches wanders among the still warm corpses

and that brave inmate of cool bins in the earth,
the soldier, lies back, a rose sprouting from his heart.
His country's burning. Graveyards rock
      thoughtfully, on fire,
surrounded by shrivelled trees and walls that perspire.

Above them burning cinders turn the skies black,
though by evening the stars come back
and the dawns crying with dew run
      towards a speechless sun.
Would the landscape answer if I asked my question?

Flowers pacing through my memories again...
Am I loitering beneath gusts of rain?
A host of women and children come down the road,
      celestial smoke overhead,
a pleated pall. Dissolving. Pale and silvered.

1940

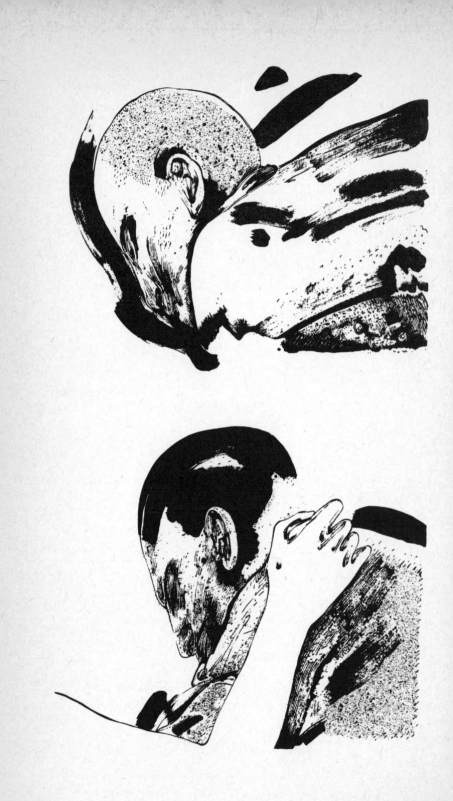

YOUR RIGHT ARM
BENEATH MY NECK

With your right arm beneath my neck I lay—
I'd asked you to hold my head, so hurt that day—
listening to your blood pulsing in the night.

It must have been midnight when I dropped off,
suddenly sunk into a gentle sleep
that rocked me back to childhood, featherlight.

You say it was nearly three in the morning
when I started with terror, sitting up
mumbling, pronouncing nonsense, shrieking in fright,

arms spread like a bird scared by some shadow
flitting through the garden, ready to take flight.
Do what? go where? which death terrified me?

You calmed me, dearest, and, sleeping sitting up,
I let you, lying silent, horror's road ahead.
And then dreamed on. Perhaps another kind of death.

6 April 1941

TO WHAT END

You're an adult now, I'd say sickened,
so confess it's useless to deny.
Come back, a voice would say to me,
just sit on the floor, talk at the sky.
As if bawling it begs, Why can't you yet?
Look, China! from the chair's leg, bearing left,
and on the right, clover, happy hunting grounds.
O, Injun pride of old, where can you be found?
don't you still care where the wind blows from?
You're getting on, writing poems, teaching...
"Just sit on the floor, talk at the sky."
And he does not sit. And he's dumb.
He's grown up, but to what end and why.

15 March 1941

SECOND ECLOGUE

PILOT
Last night we went very far, I was so mad I had to laugh,
over me their fighters droning like a flock of beehives,
and they sending a wall of flak up, firing away like hell
before our new squadron even loomed over the horizon.
We were practically cut to shreds and swept away—
yet here I am, back again! And tomorrow fearful Europe
will cower in its cellar again, scared of me...
enough about that! Written anything since yesterday?

POET
I have. Something else I can do? The cat
miaows, the dog howls, and the little fish
lovingly lays its eggs. I set it all down on paper,
for you too, so that up there you'll know the way I live
when, between blown-up and collapsing streets of houses,
the light of the bloodshot moon goes staggering,
all the city's squares bulge and fold up in terror,
breathing ceases, the sky itself is nauseated,
and the planes keep on coming, disappearing, returning,
diving like maniacs, sounding the rattles of death!
I write. Something else I can do? And how dangerous
a poem is, if you but knew, even one whimsical, delicate line,
because it also takes guts, you know: poet writing, cat
miaowing, dog howling, and the little fish—etcetera...
But what do you know? Nothing! You just hear
your engine, your ears even now crammed with its ringing.
Don't kid me: that's your friend! Joined to you.
What do you think about, flying above our heads?

81

PILOT

Go on and laugh. Up there I'm scared stiff. And I want my girlfriend
and I want to be in bed down there, with my eyes closed tight.
Or just humming through clenched teeth about her, slow and easy,
in the stuffy, wild disorder at the back of the messhall.
When aloft, I want down! and down, I want to be flying again.
This world, kneaded into clay for me, isn't home anymore.
And I know I've grown too fond of that plane,
Though we both ache to the same throbs up there...
Just that you know it! You can write it! So it won't be secret—
That I too, a destroyer, homeless now between earth and sky,
once lived, a man, a human being. Though, god! who'd know that...
Are you writing about me?

POET

                    If I live. And there's someone to write for.

27 April 1941

THIRD ECLOGUE

Country Muse, come to me now where I sit
in this drowsy cafe, the light trots by outdoors, the mole
burrows quietly below the meadow, the ground grows little humps,
and handsome, dark, white-toothed fishermen doze
on the slimed bottoms of dinghies after their morning's work.

My Country Muse, stay with me here in this urban grove,
seven salesmen may be racketing, but these seven shall not scare
                                                            you off,
their hearts right now, believe me, are loaded with care, poor guys,
and consider those on my right, legal eagles all—though not
one of them can play the flute, how well they puff at their cigars!

Be with me here! I'm teaching, and between classes I dash in
to ruminate, carried on the wings of smoke, upon love miraculous.
As the parched tree's reborn at the cockeyed twitter of a
little bird, so too was I lofted to new and old heights,
and flown to the wilds of youthful desire.

Country Muse, help me! All the horns of morning
tooting round her! in full moist tones they praise her form,
crying how her body burns, how a thin smile flits across her eyes,
how a sigh steps gangling over her lips,
how she moves, how she hugs, how she gazes at the moon!

Country Muse, help me with a love song now!
Constantly raked with sorrow as I am in this world, by fresh pain
                                                            driven,
pain always new and again! Soon I too perish here.
Here trees grow twisted, the salt mine's mouth caves in,
the brick shrieks in the wall: such when dozing are my dreams.

Country Muse, help me! The poets of this age are dying away…
the skies drop on us, no mound is raised above our ashes,
nor are they by noble, lovely Grecian urns sustained.
Yet if a poem or two of ours remains… may I write of love still?
Her body radiates towards me—O Country Muse, won't you hel

12 June 1941

FOURTH ECLOGUE

POET

If only you'd asked me as a fetus...
I knew, O I knew!
Shouting, It's barbarous! Don't want life!
Pounded dim in the dark, and slashed by light!
And I've made it. Head's been hard a long time.
All that bawling merely exercised my lungs.

VOICE

And red waves
of measles and scarlatina tossed you ashore.
The lake once tried to gulp you—and coughed you up.
Why do you suppose time has taken you in its arms after all?
and heart, liver, winged lungs,
that slimy mysterious machinery
goes right on working... well, why hasn't that obscene flower,
cancer, bloomed by now in your flesh?

POET

I was born. Protesting. Yet I'm here.
I grew up. You wonder why. Well, I've no idea.
I always wanted to be free,
but the patrol's been tracking me.

VOICE

You've walked peaks brilliant in the wind
and watched a gentle roe deer pace the slope towards night,
to where she crouched amongst the withered shrubs,
you've seen the droplet of gum on the treebole in sunlight,
a young woman stepping naked from the stream,
and once a stag beetle lit on your palm...

POET
Nowhere to be seen in captivity.
Had I been a mountain, a plant or bird…
a butterfly-thought, a solacing,
ephemeral emanation. Help me, freedom,
to find my home at last!

The peak once more, the forest, and girl, and shrubs,
and windburnt soulwings!
to be reborn in a new world,
where the light of the sun blazes up
through the golden haze of new dawns.

It's quiet, still quiet, but the storm pants,
fruit sways ripening on the branch.
The butterfly's tossed winging on the breeze.
And death blows softly through the trees.

I know now I too ripen towards death,
lifted by time's passing wave, and dropped;
prisoner that I was, my solitude grows
as the moon's rind slowly grows.

I'll be free, the earth shall let me go,
the broken world above the ground burns
smoldering. The slates are smashed.
Heavywinged imagination, soar!

VOICE
The fruit sways, and ripening drops;
memoryburdened, the deep earth will still you.
Though all things here be broken, may your fury
rise, and write on the heavens in smoke.

15 March 1943

PARIS

There's a tilt to the pavement where Boulevard
St. Michel intersects the Rue Cujas.
I've not deserted you, my wayward,
beautiful youth, even now in my heart
like an echo down a mine there's your humming voice.
The baker lived at the corner of Rue Monsieur le Prince.

And on the left, one of those great trees
in the park turned yellow against the skies
as though Autumn were something it could foresee.
Freedom, darling nymph with long thighs,
dressed in the gold of evening,
are you there yet among the veiled trees, hiding?

Summer marched along like an army,
raising dust from the road and pounding sweating,
now a cool mist followed floating by
and fragrance wafting left and right, spreading.
Through midday Summer stayed and sweet Autumn came
calling in the afternoon, a forehead wet with rain.

What a child's life I lived then,
just as I pleased, like some old pedant too,
who says, The earth is round. Such sapience.
I was still green, with beard white as snow.
Who gave a damn if I went strolling round?
I descended later below the hot ground.

Where are you, O singing stations:
CHÂTELET—CITÉ—ST. MICHEL—ODÉON!
and DENFERT-ROCHEREAU—you sound like a damnation.
The great stained wall a map blossomed on.
O where are you! I cry. I listen. Fetor
of bodies and ozone beginning to roar.

And the nights! and the pilgrimage each night
from the outlying fringe towards the Quarter!
Will that weird overcast shed its grey light
over Paris yet again at the dawn's hour
as, sodden with the writing of verse
and half-asleep, I turn towards bed and undress?

O to return! Will I find strength once more
in the deep current of my passing life?
The stinking hashhouse on the ground floor
has a tom, and he's mating on the roof.
What screeching! Will I hear that once more?
It was then I learned what a brawling uproar
Noah must have drifted through the moonlight with in
                                    days of yore.

14 August 1943

FIFTH ECLOGUE

In memory of György Bálint*

Fragment

Dear friend, how I shivered with the chill of this poem,
dreading words, avoiding them even today.
Half lines I put down,
                        trying in vain to write something else,
something else! Night, this terrible, self-concealing night
rebukes me: you must speak of him.
                                And I flinch, but the voice
has gone silent as the dead on the fields of the Ukraine out there.
You're missing.
                Nor has this autumn brought word of you.
                                        In the woods today
winter's grim oracle whispers again, heavy clouds
sweep down the sky, louring, swollen with snow.
Who knows if you're alive?
                        I neither know today nor am I any longer angered
when they shrug and cover their faces in pain.
And they know nothing.
                        But, you're alive? wounded merely?
walking through dry leaves in the rank odor of forest mud, or
are you yourself but a scent?
                            Snow's dripping over the fields now.
Missing in action. A blow, this news.
                            And the heart within thuds, freezing.
A bad, tense pain lodges between these ribs;
it quivers; the words you spoke long ago
are fresh in memory; I feel your bodily presence
like the dead—
                Yet I can't write about you today!
21 November 1943

* György Bálint (1906–1943). Writer, critic and translator of English and American
literature. He died in a field hospital in the Ukraine.

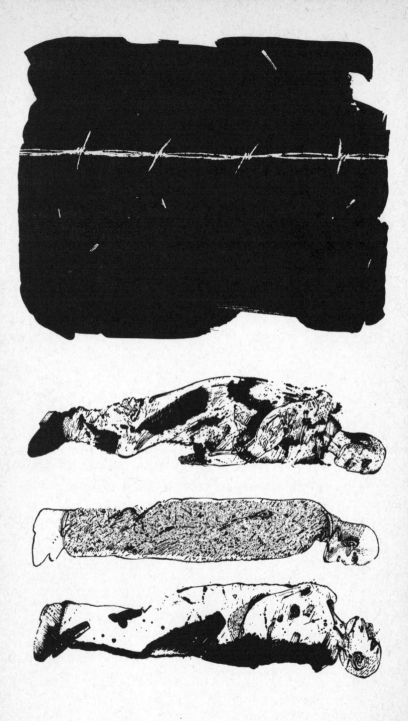

SEVENTH ECLOGUE

You see, night's coming on, and the ferocious, barbed-wire-braided
oak fence and the barracks float up, absorbed in the darkening.
The skeleton of our confinement dissolves in the torpid gaze,
and only the mind, the mind alone knows how taut the wire is.
You see, dearest, the imagination frees itself like this here too,
our crushed bodies relieved by dream, the lovely
liberator, and at such hours the camp sets off for home.

Ragged, bald, its inmates snoring fly away
from Serbia's blank attic towards hidden domestic quarters.
Hidden domestic quarters! Ah, is there such a place as home?
Not even bomb-blasted? and it still *is,* as when we went with the
army?
And this one wailing on my right, that one crumpled on my left,
will they ever make it back?
And tell me if it still is there, the land in which this
elegiac measure's understood?

Missing punctuation, just groping line after line,
I scrawl poems here in the dusk just as I live,
bleary, inching over the sheet like a caterpillar;
torch, book, everything confiscated by the *Lager*
guard, fog falling on the barracks instead of mail.

Living here among rumors and vermin, the Frenchman, the Pole,
the noisy Italian, the separatist Serb, the Jew pensive in the
mountains,
the feverish dissected body, yet all living *one* life—
waiting for good news, women's lovely words, human freedom,
for an end concealed in thickest darkness, waiting for miracles.

A captive creature among vermin, I'm lying on planks, the flea
assaults renewed again and again, though the horde of flies is res
It's night, captivity one day shorter, you see,
but so is life. Camp's asleep. The moon shines above
the landscape, the wires tightening once more by its light,
and it can be glimpsed through the window as the sentry's arm
                                                           sha
parades reflected on the wall among the sounds of the night.

The camp's asleep, you see, dearest, and dreams go rustling,
someone, startled, snorts, turns over in his narrow place and
sleeps again, his face glowing. I alone sit waking,
in my mouth a butt halfsmoked and not the savor
of your kiss, and no dream, the soothing one, comes, because
without you now I can neither die nor live.

Lager Heidenau
above Žagubica, in the mountains, July 1944

CHILDHOOD

Now the Indian froze stock still,
but up in the tree ran that hissing thrill,
the smell of gunpowder yet hovering on the wind.
On a frightened leaf two drops of blood glistened,
and an insect on the trunk did crazy callisthenics.
Twilight was redskinned. And death heroic...

25 January 1944

ROOT

Power scampers through root,
which drinks rain, eats earth,
and dreams its snow-white dream.

Through earth thrusting above earth,
climbing, and clever root is,
its arms as strong as ropes.

Vermin sleep on root's arms,
vermin squat on root's foot,
vermin infest the world.

Yet root endures down below,
gives not one damn for world,
but flowering branch alone.

Which it admires, nourishing,
sending it good flavors,
the sweet, heavenly tastes.

I'm root now myself,
lodged amongst vermin,
where this poem's been made.

Blossom I was, root become,
the dark earth weighs on me,
and my fate's fulfilled,
the saw sobs above my head.

Lager Heidenau
above Žagubica, in the mountains,
8 August 1944

À LA RECHERCHE...

You have grown lordly in remembrance too, ancient and
                                                gentle evenings!
Brilliant board wreathed by poets with their young wives,
where have you gone, slithering down the mud of the past?
Where is that night in which quickwitted friends quaffed
Gray Friar* from slender, lovely-eyed goblets?

Lines of verse sailing round the lamps' light, shining, verdant
epithets buoyed on the frothy crests of meter, and
the dead still alive, prisoners yet at home, the dear,
the lost friends, the poems made by those fallen long ago,
their hearts beneath Ukranian and Spanish and Flemish soil.

Some gritted their teeth and charged through fire,
despite themselves soldiering there,
and while the battalion slept fitfully about them, patrolled
                                                by the filthy
night, their rooms came to mind,
those islands, those caves in that society of theirs.

Some traveled in sealed cattlecars to places, or
stood unarmed in minefields, stiff with fear, or
went willingly, lugging rifles to other theaters,
silent, knowing their cause was fought for down there—
in the night now their grand dream's guarded by the angel
                                                of freedom.

* Gray Friar: Szürkebarát. A fine golden-colored white wine of Hungary.

And there were places... never mind. Where are those clever
                                        drinking-companions now?
draft notices swarmed in air, fragments of poems piled up,
crow's feet came to the sweet girls' eyes and marked their
smiling mouths; heavy and heavier those nymphs'
gliding feet in those dumbstruck years of war.

Where is that night, that tavern, that table under the lindens?
where those then still living, and those beaten down yet
                                                fighting on?
my heart hears their voices, my hand clasps theirs,
their lines come lilting to my lips, the map of their torsos
                                                    unfolds
and I measure its true scale (mute prisoner that I am)—on
                                        woeful Serbia's heights.

Where is that night, that night that never shall return,
that lies there now in death's perspective—
they shall sit at the table, lurk in women's smiles,
and sip from our glasses, though they lie unburied,
sleep in far-off forests and on foreign fields.

Lager Heidenau
above Žagubica, in the mountains, 17 August 1944

EIGHTH ECLOGUE

POET
Hail! strolling easy, you grand old man, are you borne by
                                                    wings
over the wild, mountain trail, or are you hounded?
You're winged, by passion driven, and lightning glints in
                                                    your eyes,
Hail! old man, I perceive that you must be one
of the ancient, wrathful prophets, but tell me which?

PROPHET
Which? I am Nahum, near the town of Elkosh born,
who cursed the whorish city of Nineveh the Assyrian,
a full sack of wrath, I, pouring out the holy words.

POET
Your archaic anger I know: your writing still exists.

PROPHET
Still exists. Yet wickedness now spreads wider far,
neither is the Lord's desire made known today.
For the deep rivers would run dry, said the Lord,
Carmel should stoop, Bashan and Lebanon's
glory wither, the mountain be shaken and
fire consume it all. And thus it came to pass.

POET
                    Nations rush to slaughter one another,
and the human soul is flayed, as was Nineveh.
What use fine speech, and worth what the green storm
of avid locusts? when the basest beast of all is man!

Here, there, little ones dashed against the wall,
the spire a torch, a home the oven wherein
its occupant roasts, factories going up in smoke.
The street streams folk on fire, faints with the roaring,
the bomb's bed gapes and seethes, its massive joint sprung,
and shriveling bodies are strewn in the city's squares
like dung in the pastures, and once again
everything comes to pass as in your writing. What brings you,
tell me, down from the ancient nebula to earth?

PROPHET

                  Anger. That man was and yet should be
an orphan amidst an army of heathen in human form—.
Me it shall satisfy to watch these evil cities
fall, and to witness for those to come.

POET

You've spoken once. And the Lord spoke through your words:
Woe to the stronghold bursting with booty, and its tower
raised up out of bodies; yet tell me how anger
could live for millennia in you? with such divine and stubborn
                                       flame?

PROPHET

In those long gone days, my lips deformed, like those
of sage Isaiah, were touched by the Lord with a coal: with His
                                floating ember
He searched my heart: redhot was that living coal,
held by an angel with tongs, and: "Lo, here am I, call also me
to scatter Your words abroad," I cried out after him.
And he whom once the Lord has sent can have no years,
and no repose—the coal, seraphic, glowing on his lips.
And tell me, what are thousands of years to the Lord? a moth's
                                    moment!

POET

You're so young, Father! And I am envious of you. How match
my little hour with your awful age? I am worn away,
like the rounded pebble in the rushing brook, even in my brief day.

PROPHET

So you suppose. Your last poems I know. Anger keeps you alive.
The prophet and poet's wrath are twin: meat and drink
to the people. He who would live may live thereby till
Kingdom come, as that young disciple promised,
that rabbi who fulfilled our words and the Law.
Come with me and declare the hour that is near,
the Kingdom's coming to birth. What does the Lord desire,
I asked? That Kingdom, as you can see. Come, set forth with me:
let us gather in the people. Bring your wife, and cut staves.
Fine comrade for the wanderer a staff is: look, give me that one,
and it will do for me, for I prefer a knotted one.

Lager Heidenau
above Žagubica, in the mountains, 23 August 1944

A LETTER FOR THE SPOUSE

Silent worlds dumb in the depths,
in my ear muteness shouting, I call out,
but no answer can come from remote
Serbia, prostrate in war,
and you're so far. My dream winds itself round your voice—
and I get hold of it in my heart by day,
and keep still while haughty ferns, cool to the touch,
hum rising about me.

I can't even guess when I'll see you again,
you who were so sure, solid as a psalm,
lovely as light, lovely as shadow,
to whom I could make my way blind or dumb,
I lose you in the landscape now flickering from my mind
against my field of vision;
you were real, now a dream again
sinking into the well of my adolescence

do you love me, I ask, jealous,
and will you some day, later, at the top of my youth,
will you be my mate—I'm hoping again,
drifting back along the trail of conscious being,
I know you are. My mate and my friend—
only you're so far off! Past three ferocious borders.
Autumn's coming in. Will Autumn also strand me here?
Our kisses though, how clearly I recall them;

the days I believed in miracles forgotten,
bomber squadrons passing over now;
just as I was admiring the blue of your eyes
in the sky, it grew overcast, the bombs
in the planes wanting to fall. Despite them I live—
a prisoner. I've surveyed everything
I could hope for, yet I can find my way to you;
I've traversed the soul's length for your sake—

even the routes of whole countries; over purple coals,
through falling fire I'll conjure myself through,
if I have to, but I'll get back;
tough as bark on the tree if I have to be,
and in this endless hazard I'm calmed
by the composure of men fierce in peril,
worth arms and power, cooling as waves:
soberness foursquare comes over me.

Lager Heidenau
above Žagubica, in the mountains,
August-September 1944

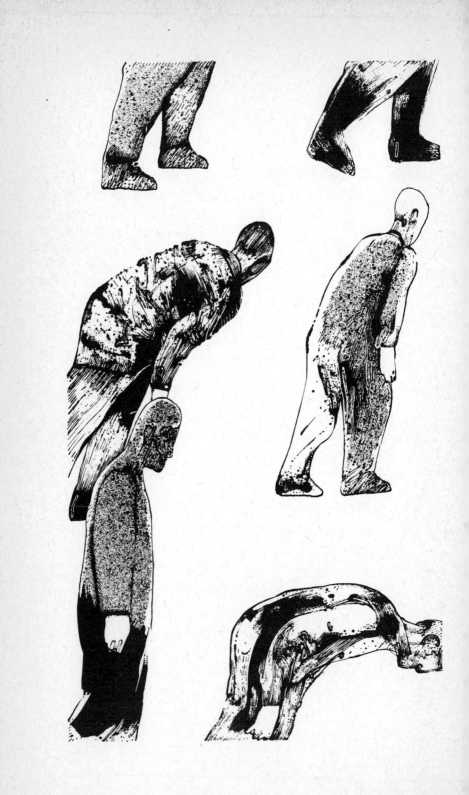

FORCED MARCH

o down, and you're crazy to get up, trudge on, and on
ke vagrant pain itself   urging ankle ahead, and knee
et moving along again   as though picked up by wings,
1 vain the ditch calls to you   you'll never risk repose in its arms
nd if you ask, Why not stay?   perhaps the answer comes. The wife,
1e waits for you, and a   sweeter, wiser death.
'hat's one clever customer: over the houses there
nly the charred wind twisting up   a good long while now,
1e side of the house flat on its back   the plum tree knocked over, and
1e hackles of household night   gone all fuzzy with fear.
.h, if I could believe: it's not just my heart holding dear
'hatever makes it worth it,   but that there is a place called home,
nd it actually exists! just as   once upon a time the honeybee of peace
'ould hum through the old, cool front porch   while plum jam cools
nd the late summer hush lies   sunning along the drowsing gardens,
'uit among the leaves   swaying nude,
nd Fanni there, blonde, waiting   by the rusted hedge,
1e languid morning slowly   scrawls its shadow—
Jait! maybe it's there for me still!   the moon's so round today!
)on't walk, off, brother!   call me, and I'm up again! once more!

or, 15 September 1944

Thick, ferocious roar of cannon rolling up from Bulgaria,
slamming into the ridge, hesitating, then falling;
man, beast, cart and thought all jammed,
the road shies whining away, the maned sky gallops off.
Amid this roiling confusion you are fixed in me,
shining in my deepest consciousness, forever still
and mute as the angel admiring the destruction,
or the beetle lodging itself in the rotting tree.

In the mountains, 30 August 1944

From here it's nine kilometers
to where stacks and houses are burning
and dumb, terrified peasants roost
puffing their pipes at the edge of the meadows.
Here the little shepherdess steps
on the pond, ruffling its surface,
and the curly flock leans over
the water's edge drinking cloud.

Červenka, 6 October 1944

---

* Razglednica: Serbo-Croatian for picture postcard. These are the last poems in the
Bor Notebook, found in the pocket of the coat on the corpse of Radnóti, exhumed
from a mass grave two years later. Radnóti had been on a forced march from a con-
centration camp in Serbia.

Bloody spittle froths from the muzzles of oxen,
people piss blood,
the company's stuck in foul, rank clots.
Hideous death blowing overhead.

Mohács, 24 October 1944

I dropped alongside him, his body rolling over,
already tightening, a cord about to snap.
Shot in the neck. You'll be finished off like this—
I muttered to myself—so just lie still.
Patience flowers into death now.
Der springt noch auf, spoken over me.
Mud and blood drying on my ear.

Szentkirályszabadja, 31 October 1944

TRANSLATOR'S NOTE

I have been translating Hungarian poetry collaboratively since 1962, but it was only after my first visit to Budapest in 1972 as a guest of the Hungarian P.E.N. Club that I undertook the challenge of putting into my words the work of the more than two dozen contemporary writers, including some who are of Radnóti's generation and knew him well. And, it was only after I had done hundreds of pages of translation that I began to work on the poems of Miklós Radnóti. The results of that effort make up this book. There have been others who have translated Radnóti, but I hope that what I have done will make him *even* more recognizable, for I have attempted to bring him over into American by preserving his stanzaic forms and patterns of rhyming, yet without adding or subtracting words and syllables in order to imitate forms and meters that, as in the case of the Eclogues, were themselves imitations and adaptations of the Classical models. Radnóti was a formal poet, to my way of understanding him, yet never a slave to his forms; that is, his language and his tone of voice, his eye and his manner of delivery, gave us a contemporary speaking voice, at times gravely colloquial and yet also informally grave. What makes him attractive and always possible is not merely the tragedy of his life and times, both of which were, it seems, complementary, but his attempt to place himself as a *European* poet, to make himself both Hungarian and international, so that he could speak for Europe itself and not be remembered just by his countrymen, who use a language that is utterly without relation to the Indo-European tongues. That his tragic end was in fact part of the international disaster of World War II is a fact that simply emphasizes his early prescience, and makes it seem as though he is certainly a poet who foresaw his destiny, and prepared himself to voice it from the beginning until mere hours before he was murdered, as his very last poems show.

I hope that he will live on in these translations. And I hope that the English-speaking world will find in these poems yet another great Continental poet whose life and work preserves the grace and greatness of art under the shadow and talons of the exterminators of humanity and its heritage of values.

I wish to express my gratitude here, too, towards my collaborator, Mária Kőrösy, who prepared the literal, raw versions of these poems in the manner I requested, and who worked patiently with me, answeing my innumerable questions about phrases and words. Mária Kőrösy is a native of Budapest who graduated as Master of Arts in English in 1972 from the University of Budapest. She is English Secretary of the Hungarian P.E.N. Club and in 1974–1975 held a British Council grant to study in London, as well as taking courses in 1977 in Victoriau Literature at the University of London. She has worked with many writers, assisting them in collaborative translating, as part of the work of the Hungarian P.E.N. Club's Program in Translation, which has been extremely generous to poets and sedulous in caring for them, under the direction of its recently-retired General Secretary, Professor László Kéry, of the Department of English, University of Budapest, ever since the late 1960s.

Jascha Kessler